PRESS ON!

A PRACTICAL GUIDE FOR FOLLOWING JESUS

DALE TALBERT

ISBN: 979-8-218-36472-4
First Edition
Printed in the United States of America

For more information, contact:
Fellowship of Montgomery
12681 FM 149
Montgomery, TX 77316
https://thefmchurch.com

Cover Design: Zach Angelo and Norma Evelyn Jackson
Illustrations: John Douglas
Project Support: Jenna Coker

To Kim and our wonderful, growing family:
Madison, Josh, Kayden, Kayson, Brayden,
Lindsey, Mallory, and Max. I love you all.

To Mom and Dad. I love you and
thank God that I am your son.

To my Fellowship of Montgomery church family. It
is truly a blessing to serve Jesus together with you.

Table of Contents

Foreword

In the ever-changing journey of life, we consistently encounter moments that demand our perseverance and inspire progress. From the earliest steps of a child to the multifaceted challenges of adulthood, each phase presents opportunities for growth. This concept of continual advancement is not just a secular experience but is deeply rooted in the Christian walk as well.

In *PRESS ON!*, Dr. Dale Talbert invites readers into a journey of spiritual growth, offering practical insights drawn from his more than 27 years in pastoral ministry. Talbert weaves together his extensive experience as a pastor, educator, and student of the Bible, presenting a narrative that is not only informative but also deeply encouraging. This book acts as a compass, leading readers toward a closer walk with the Lord and a more fulfilling spiritual life.

The title, *PRESS ON!*, evokes a sense of purposeful movement, much like my favorite hobby—hiking. Be it a leisurely walk or a challenging climb, hiking demands meticulous preparation, paralleling the journey of faith Talbert describes. Progress, whether on a mountain trail or the path to spiritual maturity, requires constant commitment and a readiness to step forward.

In *PRESS ON!*, Talbert explores fundamental Christian principles such as baptism, evangelism, the role of biblical community, and more. His advice is practical and actionable, emphasizing that true spiritual growth, similar to the rewards of a hike, is realized in the journey itself—in the living out of these principles, facing life's challenges, and finding joy in each step toward spiritual maturity.

PRESS ON! is a practical call to actively engage in our spiritual journey. It encourages us not just to learn about our faith but to put it into practice, experiencing the true depth and blessings of a life devoted to walking with Jesus Christ.

Dr. Brian Roberson
Executive Pastor
Fellowship of Montgomery

Introduction
Press On

I press on to reach the end of the race and
receive the heavenly prize for which God,
through Christ Jesus, is calling us.

–Philippians 3:14, NLT

IF LIFE IS a journey, then the question that begs to be asked is: Where am I going? As I write this, my family is navigating a season of constant change and transitions on this journey of life. College graduations, job opportunities, and marriage plans are the conversations unfolding among my family members. While many have traveled this way before, it is now our turn to walk this portion of the journey. We are deeply grateful for God's guidance and the friends and family members who are aiding us in discovering the best path forward. Every decision people make regarding issues like where to work, who to marry, or when to buy a home is important. However, the most important decision anyone can ever make is the choice to believe in Jesus Christ as their Savior.

My brother, sister, and I were blessed to grow up in a wonderful home, nurtured by our loving parents. My dad held a management position at American Airlines, while my mom was there for us every day when we came home from school. We lived a fairly normal life in a fairly normal small town. During the early years of my parents' marriage, a gentleman who lived nearby invited them to church. Nervously, they accepted, and that little church in Claremore, Oklahoma, soon became our church home. I am greatly indebted to my parents and hold deep appreciation for their concerned friend's invitation, for it was in that church that I committed my life to Jesus.

Perhaps you are reading this book because someone you know suggested it, and right about now, you might be wondering what it means to give your life to Jesus. I am so glad you do! You see, I was a young man who had grown up learning a lot about Jesus and the stories of the Bible. I attended church services frequently, participated in Bible study groups, and even volunteered to help with the children and youth. However, it did not matter how much "religious" work I did, I could not shake this feeling in my chest that something was not right between God and me. I had this fear that if my time on Earth suddenly ended, I would not go to Heaven.

Then, on March 6, 1994, something wonderful happened. Just before the Sunday morning service, the pastor of my hometown church walked up to me and said, "Dale, pay attention today." The look on my face must have been one of fear because he quickly followed up by saying, "Lighten up. I'm just playing with you."

What that pastor did not know was that I was struggling with whether or not I was even a Christian and if I would actually have a home in Heaven. I was a young man with a wonderful wife, a beautiful baby girl, a new home, and more, but something still was not right. Something was missing.

When I laid my head on my pillow at night, there was no peace in my heart. I was worried because I knew a few things about myself. I knew that I had done things in my life that the Bible calls sin, and the Bible is clear: sin separates people from God. I also knew that I would not live on this Earth forever and that anyone departing from this world without God's forgiveness would spend eternity in Hell.

You can probably understand, now, why my ears perked up as the pastor told me to pay attention. I needed to pay attention. I needed to know what God said about being forgiven of my sins and how I could have the assurance of an eternal home in Heaven.

As the pastor shared his sermon that day, I realized that there was nothing I could personally do to earn my way into Heaven. Scripture says, "No one can ever be made right with God by doing" (Romans 3:20, NLT). Even if you could live the rest of your life without sinning, you would still be guilty of the sins of the past. You, me, and everyone else on this planet have sinned, and the Bible says, "Your wrongdoings have caused a separation between you and your God" (Isaiah 59:2,

NASB). And that is the bad news… that all of us are separated from God by sin.

However, the Good News is this: God loved us too much not to make a way for us to be forgiven. That is why He sent Jesus. God's Son came to this Earth and lived a sinless life. Then, when His time here was through, Jesus allowed people to nail Him to a cross where He experienced the punishment we deserved for our sins. Jesus willingly gave His life as the one and only sacrifice God would accept for the forgiveness of our sins. Then, three days later, Jesus rose from the dead, proving He is the Son of God and is victorious over sin and death. Now, Jesus offers the free gift of His forgiveness to everyone.

Would you like to know how to receive this gift of God's forgiveness and gain an eternal home in Heaven? Jesus did all that needed to be done for you to have it, and all you need to do to receive it is to believe! In other words, place your faith in Jesus and in Him alone to be your Savior—the one and only one who can forgive you and bring you into a right relationship with God. Jesus said, "For God so loved the world that he gave his one and only Son, that whoever believes in him shall not perish but have eternal life" (John 3:16, NIV).

Are you ready to receive God's gift of forgiveness? If so, then I would encourage you to wholeheartedly pray something like this:

- God, I admit that I am a sinner.
- I recognize that my sin has separated me from You.

- I know that You love me.
- I believe that Your Son, Jesus, died on the cross for my forgiveness.
- I believe He rose from the grave so I could have eternal life.
- Now, Jesus, I am trusting in You.
- Come into my life as my Savior and forgive me of my sins.
- Thank You, God, for saving me now and forever more.
- This is my prayer in Jesus' name. Amen.

If you prayed this prayer and placed your faith in Jesus for your forgiveness, then allow me to be the first to welcome you into God's family. I would love to hear from you, pray with you, and celebrate this most significant step in your life. Please feel free to call me on my office phone at Fellowship of Montgomery: (936) 597-3949. A few minutes of your time would give us the opportunity to connect and rejoice in what Jesus has done for you.

All throughout Scripture, God's people have been on a journey. Abraham's journey took him from Ur to Canaan. Moses' journey took him from a basket on the edge of the Nile River to leading God's people out of slavery in Egypt. David's journey took him from tending sheep to ruling over Israel as its king. An outspoken fisherman, named Simon, went from catching and selling fish to catching and discipling people.

As you open the pages of this book, I want to invite

you into the most incredible journey you could ever undertake—the journey of following Jesus Christ. As with any worthwhile journey, there will be lessons to learn, new things to do, and good times to be celebrated along the way. This book is designed to help you and encourage you as, step-by-step, you advance in your journey of faith with Jesus Christ as your Savior and Lord.

Press On!
Dale

Ponder and Practice

1. **Defining the Journey's Direction:** Reflecting on the question "Where am I going?", discuss how your faith in Jesus Christ has shaped the direction of your life's journey. What major decisions have you faced, and how has your faith influenced these choices?
2. **Personal Experience of Committing to Jesus:** Share your story of how you came to commit your life to Jesus. What were the circumstances, feelings, or events that led you to this decision? How has this commitment changed the course of your life?
3. **The Importance of a Church Community:** Discuss the role of the church and Christian community in your faith journey. How has being part of a church family impacted your spiritual growth? Reflect on the significance of having friends and family who support and guide you in your faith.
4. **Understanding and Overcoming Doubts:** The introduction mentions struggling with doubts about salvation and a relationship with God.

Discuss any doubts you may have experienced in your faith journey. How did you address these doubts, and what helped you find assurance in your relationship with God?

5. **The Journey of Following Jesus:** The introduction invites readers into the journey of following Jesus Christ. What does this journey look like for you currently? Discuss the lessons you are learning, the challenges you are facing, and how you are finding joy and purpose in following Jesus.

Chapter 1

The Significance of Baptism

Go, therefore, and make disciples of all nations,
baptizing them in the name of the Father
and of the Son and of the Holy Spirit.

–Matthew 28:19, CSB

THE WAY A journey starts can have a tremendous impact on the way it ends. Even the slightest departure from the proper path can have far-reaching consequences down the line. In navigation, the impact of just one degree of deviation is profound—not at first, perhaps, but over the long haul. Imagine embarking on a flight from Houston to Hawaii. Initially, a one-degree variance off course may appear inconsequential. However, as you travel farther and farther, that seemingly minor deviation accumulates and grows. Instead of arriving at your desired destination, you will find yourself dangerously off track, heading toward a catastrophic crash into the ocean. This illustration is true not only in the realm of travel but also in the context of our spiritual journey. Starting right is of utmost importance.

As a follower of Jesus Christ, one of your very first steps of obedience after your salvation is baptism. Over the years, I have spoken with many Christians about their spiritual journey. Most mentioned a time in their life, such as youth camp or Vacation Bible School, when they placed their faith in Jesus. As the conversations continue, I listen for when and where they were baptized. Inevitably, many will admit that they never followed through with this very important step in their walk with the Lord, and this is troubling. I know how important it is for believers to obey the will of God as revealed to us in Scripture. In fact, Jesus said, "He who has My commandments and keeps them is the one who loves Me" (John 14:21, NASB). Those are not just some idle words spoken by a preacher. Those are the words of our Lord, and He said our obedience reveals something about our love for Him. So, what message has your obedience regarding believer's baptism been communicating to Jesus?

Before returning to Heaven, Jesus stood in the presence of His closest friends and followers on a mountaintop in Galilee. He knew this was a mission-critical moment and not a time for small talk. Only the most important details needed to be spoken, and Jesus chose to instruct them by saying, "Go, therefore, and make disciples of all nations, baptizing them in the name of the Father and of the Son and of the Holy Spirit, teaching them to observe everything I have commanded you.

And remember, I am with you always, to the end of the age" (Matthew 28:19-20, CSB).

When my family and I travel for vacation, we always have a few tasks that need to be done at our home while we are away. Thankfully, we have good friends who are always glad to take care of these chores in our absence. The list usually includes responsibilities such as picking up the mail, watering the plants, and taking care of the pets. These are what the Talbert family considers to be mission-critical tasks that must be done, and we trust our friends to follow our instructions completely.

As Jesus stood there with His disciples, preparing to return to Heaven, He could have spoken with them regarding a multitude of topics. He could have explained to them exactly what happened to dinosaurs, why He made mosquitos, or elaborated on a thousand other topics, but none of those details were what He chose to talk about. Instead, Jesus used those important moments to talk about what He considered to be mission-critical, and one of the topics He addressed was the importance of baptism. Now, please understand that if baptism was important enough for Jesus to talk about at that moment, then surely, we need to discuss and understand its significance today.

Who Should Be Baptized?

Baptism is an act of obedience that is only for those who have placed their faith in Jesus Christ as their Savior. Over time, some have erroneously taught that baptism is an activity that results in or completes a person's salvation. Frequently, those who hold to this misunderstanding point to Peter's words in Acts 2:38, where he said, "Repent and be baptized, each of you, in the name of Jesus Christ for the forgiveness of your sins" (Acts 2:38, CSB).

Those who teach that baptism is required for salvation are assuming that the word translated "for" in this verse means "in order to receive." In other words, "be baptized in order to gain your salvation." However, the original Greek word "eis" that is translated into our English language by the word "for" can also mean "because of," which is the case in Acts 2:38.

Think about it like this: When you tell someone, "Take two aspirin for your headache," it is obvious to everyone that you do not mean for them to take two aspirin in order to get (or acquire) a headache. What you are saying, instead, is to take two aspirin *because* they have a headache. And that is how this passage in Acts is to be understood and applied. Peter is saying, "Be baptized, each of you, in the name of Jesus Christ [because you already have] the forgiveness of your sins" (Acts 2:38, CSB).

Furthermore, Peter's next sermon, recorded in Acts 3:12-26, offers additional insight into the role of baptism. Here, Peter emphasizes repentance and turning to God without any mention of baptism. This is particularly noteworthy given the proximity of this sermon to his earlier one. If baptism were a crucial requirement for salvation, it would be reasonable to expect Peter to consistently include it in his preaching, especially since the messages were delivered to a similar audience within a short timeframe of each other. The omission of baptism in this context suggests that while it is a significant act of obedience for believers, it is not a mandatory component for salvation.

Later, in Acts 20:21, the Apostle Paul confirms the message preached by Peter regarding salvation through faith in Jesus. Paul states, "I have declared to both Jews and Greeks that they must turn to God in repentance and have faith in our Lord Jesus" (Acts 20:21, NIV). As Paul writes about the pathway to experiencing God's forgiveness, he does not mention baptism or any other requirement besides faith in Jesus Christ.

God gave baptism as a symbol of two very important truths. First, going under the water and being raised up signifies your belief in the death, burial, and resurrection of Jesus Christ. Secondly, baptism represents the transformation that has occurred in your life through conversion. It symbolizes dying to your old sinful self, burying it in baptism, and being raised to live a new life in Jesus Christ. It is important to understand that baptism does not contribute to your salvation (Ephesians 2:8-9). Rather, you are baptized *because* you have already been saved.

When Should a Person Be Baptized?

My answer to the question of when a person should be baptized is always the same: as soon as you can after becoming a Christian. In Acts 2, the Bible tells of a time when Peter preached the Good News about Jesus to a crowd that had gathered in Jerusalem for a special celebration. As the people listened, they became convinced that Peter's message was true, that Jesus is Lord. As a result, 3,000 placed their faith in Jesus that day. Then, what did these new Christians do? The Bible says, "So those who accepted his message were baptized, and that day about 3,000 people were added to them" (Acts 2:41, CSB).

The biblical example is one of salvation soon followed by obedience in baptism. I am convinced that a new Christian's willingness to be baptized as quickly as possible is a strong indicator of the kind of Christian life they will live. If a person is willing to be baptized right away, they are on the right path of rapid obedience to the commands of the Savior.

From time to time, I encounter those who hold the erroneous belief that infants should also be baptized. However, nowhere is this practice taught in the Bible. Baptism always follows a person's salvation, and this is the order we see lived out by the early Christians in the New Testament. In fact, the only examples of baptism found in Scripture are those of people who were old enough to make this decision of their own free will. Each person being baptized in the Bible was old enough to comprehend its meaning and to make the choice personally to follow through with baptism or not.

How Should a Believer Be Baptized?

The proper, biblical mode of baptism is immersion. Only immersion gives us an incredible visualization of Jesus' death, burial, and resurrection. One compelling reason for baptizing by immersion is the fact that "the Greek word for baptism in the New Testament means 'to immerse' or 'to dip,' implying that the candidate was plunged beneath the water."[1] Even early denominational leaders practiced and made statements in support of baptism by immersion. Consider the following:

- Martin Luther (Lutheran) wrote, "Baptism, then, signifies two things—death and resurrection; that is, full and complete justification. I would have the candidates for baptism completely immersed in water, as the word says and as the sacrament signifies. Not that I deem this necessary, but it were well to give to so perfect and complete a thing a perfect and complete sign; thus it was also doubtless instituted by Christ."[2]
- John Calvin (Presbyterian) wrote, "It is evident that the term *baptise* means to immerse, and that this was the form used by the primitive Church."[3]

---

[1] Herbert Lockyer, Sr., ed., *Illustrated Bible Dictionary*, s.v. "Baptism" (Nashville: Thomas Nelson, 1986), 134.

[2] Martin Luther, *Luther's Three Treatises* (Moscow, ID: Canon Press, 2021), 153-154.

[3] John Calvin, *Institutes Of The Christian Religion, Book Fourth* (Houston: V Solas Press, 2021), 323.

- In John Wesley's (Methodist) commentary on Romans 6:4, he wrote, "'We are buried with him'—Alluding to the ancient manner of baptizing by immersion."[4] Wesley also said, "I believe (myself) it is a duty to observe, so far as I can (without breaking communion with my own Church)... To baptize by immersion."[5] Regarding Wesley's practice, it is said that, "When Mr. Wesley baptized adults, professing faith in Christ, he chose to do it by trine immersion, if the persons would submit to it, judging this to be the Apostolic method of baptizing."[6]
- James Gibbons (Roman Catholic) said, "For several centuries after the establishment of Christianity baptism was usually conferred by immersion; but since the twelfth century the practice of baptizing by infusion has prevailed in the Catholic Church, as this manner is

---

[4] John Wesley, *John Wesley's Notes On Paul's Epistle To The Romans* (Nashville: Methodist Evangelistic Materials, 1962), 34.

[5] John Wesley, *John Wesley*, edited by A. C. Outler (Oxford University Press, Incorporated, 1980), 13, accessed June 28, 2023, ProQuest Ebook Central, http://ebookcentral.proquest.com/lib/liberty/detail.action?docID=684619.

[6] Henry Moore, *Life of the Reverend John Wesley, A.M., fellow of Lincoln College, Oxford* (New-York: N. Bangs and J. Emory, 1824; J. & J. Harper and A. Hoyt imprint), 1:425, accessed June 28, 2023, https://go.gale.com/ps/i.do?p=SABN&u=vic_liberty&id=GALE|CY0111260895&v=2.1&it=r&sid=summon.

> attended with less inconvenience than baptism by immersion."[7]

In the first chapter of Mark's Gospel, we read about the baptism of Jesus. The Bible informs us that "In those days Jesus came from Nazareth in Galilee and was baptized in the Jordan by John. As soon as he came up out of the water, he saw the heavens being torn open and the Spirit descending on him like a dove" (Mark 1:9-10, CSB).

Clearly, for someone to come up out of the water, they must first go down under the water. Based on Jesus' example, the definition of the word, and the practice of the early church, it is clear that the proper method for baptizing a follower of Jesus is by immersion.

So, what about you? Have you placed your faith in Jesus as your Savior? If so, have you been baptized by immersion? Remember, small deviations off course can have detrimental effects on the journey. Baptism will not save anyone, but Christians who are unwilling to obey Jesus in this important step may not experience the abundant growth and blessings God has planned for their future.

---

[7] James Gibbons, "The Faith Of Our Fathers," *The Project Gutenberg*, 2008, accessed May 12, 2023, https://www.gutenberg.org/cache/epub/27435/pg27435-images.html.

Ponder and Practice

1. **Understanding Baptism:** Explore how baptism symbolizes the death, burial, and resurrection of Jesus Christ. Discuss why these symbols are significant in a believer's life. What personal insights or changes in perception have you experienced regarding baptism?
2. **Obedience and Timing in Baptism:** Analyze why prompt baptism after accepting Christ is emphasized. How might delaying baptism affect a believer's spiritual journey and growth?
3. **Baptism and Salvation:** Discuss the misconception that baptism is a requirement for salvation using insights from Acts 2:38 and Ephesians 2:8-9. Explore the potential risks associated with misunderstanding the true nature and purpose of baptism. How can this knowledge shape your discussions with others about baptism and faith?
4. **The Proper Method of Baptism:** Reflect on why immersion is presented as the correct mode of baptism in this chapter. How does this approach align with the symbolism of Jesus' death, burial, and resurrection?

5. **Personal Reflection and Commitment:** Reflect on the details of your baptism, including when, where, and how it occurred. Share how this experience has been significant in your walk with Christ. For any believer who has not yet been baptized, consider when you might schedule your baptism. Share this decision with another Christian for encouragement and accountability.

Chapter 2
Sharing Your Faith with Others

Therefore, we are ambassadors for Christ, as though God were making an appeal through us; we beg you on behalf of Christ, be reconciled to God.

–2 Corinthians 5:20, NASB

IT HAS OFTEN been said that there is at least one thing Christians and non-Christians have in common: They both get nervous when you talk about evangelism. Over the years, I have found this to be true. If I bring up the topic of sports, it often leads to a lively discussion, regardless of the other person's interests. Even if they have limited knowledge of the game or team, they usually listen politely or share what they know. However, if they are truly passionate about the sport or team in question, ending the conversation might become a challenge.

This is not the case with the topic of evangelism. Just mentioning words like "witnessing" or "sharing your testimony" causes most people to promptly change the topic or end the conversation altogether.

In a survey conducted with over 2,000 individuals who identified as born-again Christians, they were asked about their belief in having a personal responsibility to share the Gospel with others. Seventy-three percent answered "yes," believing that Christians are responsible for sharing the saving message of Jesus with those who are lost. The follow-up question then inquired about the number of respondents who had actually shared the Gospel in the previous twelve months. Only fifty-two percent reported sharing the message of Jesus within that timeframe.[8]

Every Christian needs to understand that refusing to share Jesus Christ with people who are lost is a sin. How do we know this? Because the Bible says, "Whoever knows the right thing to do and fails to do it, for him it is sin" (James 4:17, ESV). Therefore, if we are aware that pointing someone to Jesus is the right thing to do and we choose not to, then it is a sin—specifically, a sin of omission.

Think about it like this: Imagine you are on vacation in Arizona, and you decide to drive over to see the Grand Canyon. The beauty of God's creation is truly amazing, and the canyon is so grand that it is impossible to take it

---

[8] David Kinnaman, "Is Evangelism Going Out of Style?" Barna, accessed February 16, 2022, https://www.barna.com/research/is-evangelism-going-out-of-style/.

all in. Suppose you are standing near a couple of sightseers who are caught up in conversation and the souvenirs they purchased and neither one notices that they are walking dangerously close to the edge of the canyon. What would you do? Would you turn and walk away in an effort to put distance between you and the inevitable tragedy, or would you speak up and warn those who are in danger? I hope all of us would say something quickly, boldly, and lovingly to warn them and guide them to a place of safety.

Each day, we come across individuals in various settings such as our homes, offices, carpools, the sideline of our kid's soccer practice, and elsewhere who have yet to accept Jesus as their Savior. Unfortunately, there are numerous instances when we remain silent or say very little to assist them. We fail to engage in conversations about our faith or seize opportunities to invite them to church, effectively allowing them to continue approaching the brink of a perilous cliff. And the reality is that a fate far worse than falling to the bottom of a canyon awaits those who never place their faith in Jesus.

Our loving God does not want anyone to be separated from Him or to suffer for eternity in Hell. That is why He sent His Son, Jesus, as the sacrifice for our sins. Jesus did His part, and now God wants us to do our part by sharing the Good News of Jesus with others.

I recognize that there may be someone reading this book who is thinking, "God could never use someone like me." Friend, that is simply not true. God desires to and is fully capable of using you if you are willing to let

Him. Throughout the Bible, we come across story after story of God utilizing ordinary people, just like you and me, to accomplish amazing things. They were not flawless individuals, but they placed their trust in God and attempted great things for Him. And that is the mindset all Christians should adopt today—to trust God and try great things for Him.

While sharing the message of Jesus with others is indeed crucial, it is not something God will make you do. Just as Jesus did not force His way into your life, He will not force anyone to share His message with others. Nevertheless, all believers should willingly take it upon themselves to tell someone about Jesus, and here are three reasons why.

#1 – Jesus Tells Us to Tell Others

The first reason we must share the Gospel with others is because Jesus commands His followers to spread the word about Him. In the opening chapter of the book of Acts, Luke recorded some of our Savior's final words on Earth. Jesus said, "But you will receive power when the Holy Spirit comes upon you. And you will be my witnesses, telling people about me everywhere—in Jerusalem, throughout Judea, in Samaria, and to the ends of the earth" (Acts 1:8, NLT).

As we reflect on Jesus' words, it becomes evident that He is not merely offering a suggestion. This moment with His disciples was of utmost importance, focusing on essential information. And what did Jesus instruct

His followers to do after He departed? Jesus emphasized that every Christian, those alive back then and those alive today, is meant to be His witness.

But what does it mean to be a witness? Simply put, a witness is someone who shares their firsthand experiences. In legal cases, for instance, a witness is expected to provide testimony based on their personal knowledge and observations. As a Christian, you are already a witness to the life-transforming power of Jesus Christ. You possess personal knowledge of how your life was before encountering Jesus, how you received God's forgiveness through faith, and the subsequent changes that have occurred in your life. This makes you a credible witness!

However, as significant as this is, there is even more that God has done to assist you. When Jesus ascended to Heaven, He did not leave His people powerless and alone. This is precisely the message Jesus was conveying when He said, "You will receive power when the Holy Spirit comes upon you" (Acts 1:8, NLT).

After Jesus returned to Heaven, He sent the Holy Spirit to dwell within every person who places their faith in Him. One of the incredible roles of the Holy Spirit is to assist and empower us in sharing God's message of salvation through faith in Jesus. So, whenever you endeavor to tell someone about Jesus, the good news is that you are not alone. The Holy Spirit is present to guide your words and help the other person understand.

#2 - God Loves People

Another very important reason why Christians must share the message of Jesus is because of God's love for people. Most of us are familiar with John 3:16. In this passage, Jesus said, "For God loved the world so much that he gave his one and only Son, so that everyone who believes in him will not perish but have eternal life" (John 3:16, NLT).

Whom did Jesus say God loves? He said God loves the world. Now, think about this: When you reach the end of that verse, do you see any exclusions? No! There is nothing to indicate that anyone is left out of God's love. God loves the world, and that includes you, me, the obnoxious fans of that team you always cheer against, and even the person you saw on the news in a far-off land shouting threats at our nation. God loves everyone!

But God did not merely talk about His great love for us. God acted! God moved! God reached out to save us by sending His Son, Jesus. And since our God is active in demonstrating His love for the world, we should be active as well. How do we know this? Well, in 1 Peter 2:21, the Word of God says, "[Jesus] is your example, and you must follow in his steps" (1 Peter 2:21, NLT).

So, how are we doing? Are we following in Jesus' footsteps and actively sharing the message of salvation with those around us, or are we holding it all inside? Are we guilty of keeping the Good News about God's love and forgiveness all to ourselves?

#3 – People Are Lost Without Jesus

Let me ask you a question: Are you a perfect person? Obviously, the answer is no. Do you know anyone in this world who is perfect? Again, the answer is no.

Why? It is because all of us have sinned. All of us have lied, cheated, and in one way or another, broken God's commandments. In fact, the book of James tells us, "For the person who keeps all of the laws except one is as guilty as a person who has broken all of God's laws" (James 2:10, NLT). So, clearly, everyone is guilty of disobedience and breaking God's laws, which is the very definition of sin.

But why is it important to be aware of this? What impact does sin have on people? Looking at Romans 6:23 (NET), the Bible tells us that "the payoff of sin is death."

Think of it like this: Every day when you go to work, you earn something—a paycheck. This same concept applies when it comes to our sin. We receive something in return. However, the paycheck for sin is not something to look forward to. The consequence of sin is death, and this does not solely refer to physical death on this Earth. It primarily signifies eternal suffering and separation from God and Heaven, as described in this verse.

But thank God that He did not stop with only giving us the bad news. He also provided us with a solution by giving us the Savior. When we read Romans 6:23 in its entirety, we see that it goes on to say, "The payoff of sin is death, but the gift of God is eternal life in Christ Jesus our Lord" (Romans 6:23, NET).

And that is the Good News that God wants everyone to hear and believe—that by trusting in Jesus, you can have all of your sins forgiven and receive an eternal home in Heaven. However, this can only happen through a personal relationship with Jesus Christ.

Everyone Can Share the Good News

One of the major barriers preventing many people from sharing the message of salvation is the feeling of not being prepared. While I know it is possible for everyone to be a witness by simply sharing their own salvation story (see Appendix A for help with writing your personal salvation story), I also believe it is helpful to be familiar with an outline or plan that can be utilized when needed. One plan I highly recommend becoming familiar with is a variation of "The Four Spiritual Laws" (Appendix B), which is an outline I use frequently.

A second plan I would suggest for sharing the Gospel with others involves weaving the message of salvation into a relatable story. "Shifting from giving an evangelistic presentation to having an evangelistic conversation takes pressure off the witness and relates the Gospel more clearly to an unbeliever."[9] One example of doing this is by using a story I have named *Lost and Found.*

---

[9] Alvin L. Reid, *Sharing Jesus without Freaking Out* (Nashville: B&H Academic, 2017), 41.

As I share this story below, keep in mind the fact that most people like dogs, and my family is no exception. Madison has Denim and Hoss. Brayden has Honcho. Mallory has Rascal. My wife, Kim, well… she has me. And something that everyone who has a pet knows is that, eventually, these animals that we love try to break free and run off. Since this is true, I believe most people can easily relate to the following story I tell about a lost dog being found.

Lost and Found

In this example, I will use my son and his dog. If you do not have a dog, you could begin your version of this story by simply saying you know someone who had this experience with their dog. However, if you do have a dog, personalize it to fit your situation. Here's the story:

> *My son, Brayden, has a British Labrador named Honcho. Brayden loves that dog and takes Honcho with him everywhere he goes. Recently, on one of their outings, something troubling happened—Honcho got lost. He was playing and walking with Brayden in the park, and then, suddenly, he ran off. So, what did my son do? He searched and searched for Honcho. Why? Because he loves that dog and does not want him to be lost or get hurt.*
>
> *With great determination, Brayden went out searching for Honcho, and after several hours the lost dog was found. As soon as my son saw him, Brayden*

called out to him, "Honcho! Come here. Let's go home." Immediately, the dog ran to my son, who scooped up Honcho and carried him home.

Of course, the dog did not have to do this. Honcho could have chosen to stay out there all on his own, lost and separated from his master, but he made the best decision: Honcho ran to Brayden.

You may not realize it, but we are a lot like that dog. How? Well, just as the dog was lost and separated from its master, we too are lost and separated from God because of our sin. The Bible tells us that our sin creates a separation between us and God (Isaiah 59:2), and no one guilty of sin can enter into God's Kingdom (1 Corinthians 6:9).

But the good news is this: God loves us and does not want anyone to be lost and separated from Him in eternity (John 3:16). God wants us to be forgiven and to have an eternal home in Heaven with Him (2 Peter 3:9). And just like my son went out searching for his lost dog, Jesus came to Earth to seek and save people who are lost, separated from God, and headed for Hell (Luke 19:10).

Jesus came to this world, lived a sinless life, and then died on the cross as the one and only sacrifice God would accept for the forgiveness of our sins (1 Corinthians 15:1-4). Through His death and resurrection, Jesus made it possible for us to be forgiven and have an eternal home in Heaven with Him (1 Peter 3:18).

And just like there was only one way for Honcho to get home, that is, through my son, the same is true for people. There is only one way for us to be forgiven and to have an eternal home in Heaven—and that is through faith in God's Son, Jesus (John 14:6).

And just like Honcho had a choice to make whenever my son called out to him, you also have a choice to make. You can choose to remain lost, unforgiven, and separated from God and His Kingdom forever. Or you can run to Jesus, place your faith in Him, and receive God's forgiveness (2 Corinthians 6:2).

Jesus is calling out to everyone, saying, "Come to Me. I love you, and I want to forgive you. I will take care of you now and forever if you will place your faith in Me" (Matthew 11:28; Galatians 2:16).

Friend, are you ready to receive God's forgiveness? Are you ready to trust in Jesus as your Savior and follow Him as your Lord? If you are, then I would encourage you to pray something similar to this: "Dear God, I am a sinner, and I admit that my sin has separated me from You. I believe that Jesus died on the cross for my sins and rose again. I turn away from the sin that has separated me from You. Please forgive me. I place my faith in Jesus as my Savior, and I will follow Him as my Lord. Thank You for Your love, and thank You for Your forgiveness. In Jesus' name I pray. Amen."

The above is simply an example of how I have tried to work the Gospel into a relatable story. Sometimes, this might help, and at other times you may need to take a different approach. Whatever method you feel led to use, always be careful that your story does not interfere with or distract from the primary message, which is the Gospel of Jesus Christ.

The Bridge to Salvation

Another conversational approach to sharing the message of Jesus involves using an illustration known as The Bridge to Salvation. This simple drawing can be used in front of a crowd on a whiteboard or in a one-on-one setting with a friend on a napkin. There are several variations of this illustration you can consider, but I have found the following example to be helpful for me.

To begin with, take a napkin and on the left side draw a cliff. On the right side, draw another cliff being sure to leave a gap between the two. On the left cliff, draw a stick figure and say, "This represents you." Then on the right side, write the word "God" (Diagram A). As you do, say the following: "Here is God in Heaven who is perfect and holy. And one of the first things you need to know about God is that He loves you very much." Write "God Loves You" above the stick figure. Now say, "In John 3:16, (NLT), Jesus said that 'God loved the world.' And since you're in this world, that means that God loves you."

Diagram A

Then, at the bottom of the gap, write the word "Sin" (Diagram B), and say the following: "However, all of us have a problem. All of us have sinned, and sin separates us from God. The Bible tells us in Isaiah 59:2 (NASB) that 'Your wrongdoings,' i.e. sins, 'have caused a separation between you and your God.' And if a person leaves this Earth in that separated and unforgiven condition, then that is how they will spend eternity—separated from God and His Heaven in a very real place called Hell."

Diagram B

Then write the words "Bible," "Church," and "Do Good" next to the left-hand cliff (Diagram C), and say the following: "Some people think they can get to God by reading the Bible, going to church, or by being a good person, but here's the problem: none of our good works will ever be good enough to earn our way into Heaven. In fact, God's Word tells us that "No one can ever be made right with God by doing what the law commands" (Romans 3:20, NLT).

Diagram C

Now ask, "So how can a person be forgiven? How can anyone get to God and be blessed with an eternal home in Heaven?" Between the two cliffs, draw a cross bridging from one side to the other (Diagram D) and say the following: "This is why Jesus came to Earth. God's Word, in 1 Peter 3:18 (NLT) says, 'Christ suffered for our sins once for all time. He never sinned, but he died for sinners to bring you safely home to God.' Friend, Jesus lived a sinless life and died on the cross as the one and only, perfect sacrifice God would accept for the forgiveness of our sins. Now, Jesus offers the free gift of His forgiveness to everyone who will place their faith in Him as Savior."

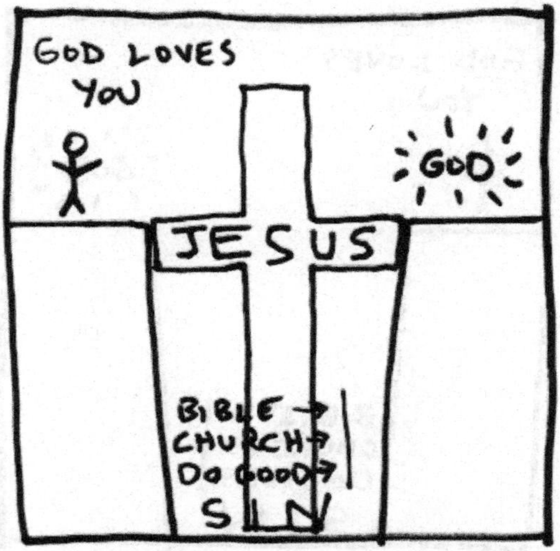

Diagram D

Then draw a dotted line from the stick figure on the left to God (Diagram E) and ask something similar to the following questions: "Would you like to know that all of your sins have been forgiven? Would you like to know that you have an eternal home in Heaven? Would you like to experience God's love and blessings, both now and for all of eternity?"

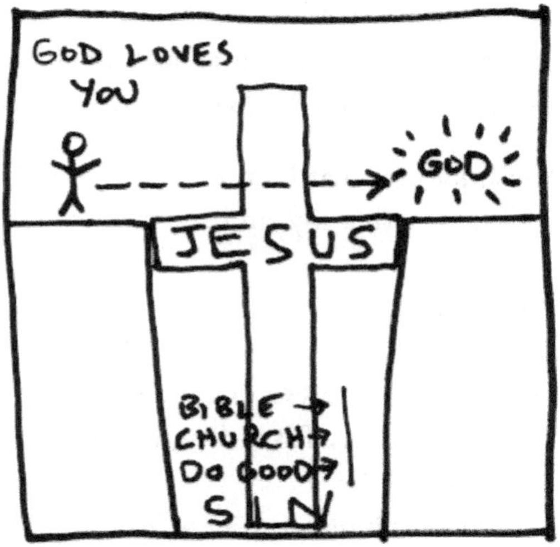

Diagram E

If the individual says yes, then say the following: "The Bible tells us, 'If you confess with your mouth, "Jesus is Lord," and believe in your heart that God raised him from the dead, you will be saved'" (Romans 10:9, NIV).

Follow this up by asking, "Do you believe Jesus died and rose again for your forgiveness? Are you ready to trust in Him as your Savior and follow Him as your Lord?"

If the individual is ready, then say, "The Bible tells us that 'Everyone who calls on the name of the Lord will be saved'" (Romans 10:13, CSB). Say, "If you are ready to trust in Jesus as your Savior, then why don't you pray right now and tell Him."

At this point, you can let the individual pray a prayer of confession and commitment on their own, or you can ask if they would like you to help by leading them in a prayer. If the person wants you to lead them, you can have them echo you in the following prayer by saying:

- God, I admit that I am a sinner.
- I recognize that my sin has separated me from You.
- I know that You love me.
- I believe that Your Son, Jesus, died on the cross for my forgiveness.
- I believe He rose from the grave so I could have eternal life.
- Now, Jesus, I am trusting in You.
- Come into my life as my Savior and forgive me.
- Thank You, God, for saving me now and forever more.
- This is my prayer in Jesus' name. Amen.

After you lead someone in praying this prayer, it is important to provide assurance of their salvation using Scripture such as Romans 8:38-39, Romans 10:13, and 1 John 5:12-13. These verses will help assure the individual of their new life in Christ. Additionally, invite this person to join you at church the following Sunday for worship, where they can continue to grow in their faith and connect with other believers.

To support their spiritual growth, seek to set up one or more follow-up conversations where you can assist this new believer in understanding some foundational beliefs (Appendix C). These conversations will help grow the individual's knowledge of God's Word and provide guidance as they embark on this new journey with Jesus. Ensure the new believer has a Bible and regularly pray for them. Provide a copy of this book as a resource to further their understanding and application of God's Word.

Ponder and Practice

1. **Challenges in Evangelism:** Reflect on the discomfort associated with evangelism for both Christians and non-Christians. Share personal experiences in sharing your faith and how you have managed any nervousness or hesitation. What steps can you take to become more comfortable and effective in evangelism?
2. **Responsibility and Action in Evangelism:** Examine the gap between acknowledging the responsibility to share the Gospel and actually doing so. What barriers might prevent Christians from evangelizing, despite their belief in its importance?
3. **Understanding Sin and the Necessity of Evangelism:** This chapter emphasizes sin as a universal problem and the role of evangelism in addressing this. Discuss how understanding the consequences of sin can motivate believers to share their faith. How does this awareness affect your perspective on the urgency and importance of evangelism?

4. **Personal Witnessing and the Holy Spirit:** Examine the role of a believer's personal testimony in evangelism. How can your personal experiences with Christ assist your evangelistic efforts? Discuss the ways in which the Holy Spirit can guide and empower your efforts to share the Gospel. Plan to share your testimony with someone as a practical step in your evangelistic journey.
5. **Personal Action Plan:** Reflect on the effectiveness of various evangelistic methods, such as relatable stories or The Bridge to Salvation. How might you incorporate these into your approach? Share your experiences with specific evangelistic tools or strategies. Identify someone in your life who may need to hear the Gospel and devise a plan for sharing it in a loving and impactful way.

Chapter 3

The Importance of Biblical Community

All the believers devoted themselves to the apostles' teaching, and to fellowship, and to sharing in meals (including the Lord's Supper), and to prayer.

–Acts 2:42, NLT

ON APRIL 5, 1976, billionaire Howard Hughes died in Houston, Texas. Soon after his passing, the public relations director for the Howard Hughes Corporation requested that the casinos in Las Vegas, where Hughes owned property, observe a minute of silence out of respect. For what was described as an uncomfortable sixty seconds, the normally noisy buildings stood silent. Eventually, a pit boss looked at his watch, then looked around at the people and said, "Okay, roll the dice. He's had his minute."[10]

---

[10] James Phelan, *Howard Hughes: The Hidden Years* (New York: Random House, 1976), 201.

Sadly, many Christians treat Jesus and His church in a manner similar to how the pit boss treated Howard Hughes. They reluctantly interrupt their plans on Sunday to attend a church service within a designated timeframe. Throughout the service, they frequently check their watches, eagerly anticipating when the allotted time will end. As soon as they can, they rush out the door, swiftly returning to their everyday lives. For these Christians, church has become a ritualistic event, attended solely out of obligation or pressure, with little genuine personal engagement.

However, it is important that every Christian understand this fundamental truth: While the church benefits from your active participation, it is equally true that as an individual, you have a deep and profound need for the church in your life.

The Church Is a Place of Family

As you read through the New Testament, you begin to realize that one of the greatest gifts Jesus gave us, after our salvation and the indwelling of the Holy Spirit, is the gift of our brothers and sisters in Christ—our church family. Oh, sure, there are other clubs and civic organizations that you can choose to belong to and enjoy, but there is no other group as important or impactful as the local church. Therefore, if, in your busy schedule, you have to make a choice between being committed to a church family or to some other group, you should always choose to be committed to the church.

Something very important to keep in mind as you search your community for the perfect church family is this: Just like there are no perfect biological families, there are no perfect church families either. Both are made up of imperfect people. The good news, however, is that in your church family, there are people of all ages who have been transformed by placing their faith in Jesus (2 Corinthians 5:17). As a result, they are a work in progress—growing to become more and more like Jesus in the way they think, speak, and behave toward God and other people.

When you become a member of a church family, you will get to know other Christians who will also get to know you. As you get to know those in your spiritual family, you will learn about one another's successes and struggles. There will be times when you can help other people in your church, and there will be times when they will seek to help you. You will find yourself praying for others during their difficult moments, and they will do the same for you. There will be those special instances when God uses you to bring His comfort to someone in your church family who is hurting. Then there will also be times when God directs someone else to be a source of comfort and encouragement for you.

A few years ago, I went through an unusually stressful period in my life. One afternoon, I started experiencing pain in my chest, shoulder, and arm, which raised concerns about my well-being. I decided to call my wife, who was away at the time, and she strongly recommended that I head to the emergency room immediately. Now, if you know me, you are aware that I tend to avoid medical visits (a habit I acknowledge is not a healthy one). I tried to convince myself that the discomfort was due to tension or perhaps a muscle strain from a recent workout. However, there was a major problem with that excuse—I had not been working out.

As the day progressed, my discomfort grew increasingly unbearable. However, despite my wife's persistent pleas, I adamantly refused to go to the emergency room. Then, around 9:00 PM, there came a knock on the side door of our home. It was a friend from our church. My wife had contacted him and described my condition, and without any hesitation, he jumped into his truck and drove straight to my house. After throwing out my best excuses and attempting to justify my decision to stay home, I realized that my friend was determined to take me to the hospital, and he was not leaving my home without me.

Praise the Lord, my heart checked out okay. Following a battery of tests and an overnight hospital stay, the doctor advised me to reduce my stress and to actually start exercising. Filled with a deep sense of gratitude, I made my way back home.

Over the next several days, my thoughts frequently revolved around two important matters. First, I needed to take better care of my health. God has blessed me with this body to use for His purposes while I am here on this Earth, and I cannot fully do that if I fail to take care of my health. Then, secondly, I was reminded of just how wonderful it was to belong to a church family and to have a brother in Christ who not only said he would help but also actually showed up and helped. That is the kind of Christian Jesus was instructing His people to be when He said, "I give you a new command: Love one another. Just as I have loved you, you are also to love one another" (John 13:34, CSB).

The Church Is a Place of Formation

One of my favorite Old Testament characters to read about, discuss, and preach on is Moses. From his birth to the end of his time on Earth, Moses teaches us so much about what to do and what not to do. Looking specifically at Exodus 2, we read this:

> *When Pharaoh heard about this, he tried to kill Moses. But Moses fled from Pharaoh and went to live in the land of Midian, and sat down by a well.*
>
> *Now the priest of Midian had seven daughters. They came to draw water and filled the troughs to water their father's flock. Then some shepherds arrived and drove them away, but Moses came to their rescue and watered their flock. When they returned to their father... he asked, "Why have you come back so quickly today?" They answered, "An Egyptian rescued us from the shepherds. He even drew water for us and watered the flock."*
>
> *"So where is he?" he asked his daughters. "Why then did you leave the man behind? Invite him to eat dinner."*

Moses agreed to stay with the man, and he gave his daughter Zipporah to Moses in marriage. –Exodus 2:15-21, CSB

If you are familiar with the story of Moses, you know that he ended up in his current situation after murdering an Egyptian whom he saw beating a Hebrew slave. To save his own life, Moses had to flee. This former prince, who had once resided in a palace with servants catering to his every need, now found himself alone and in the desert, approximately 285 miles away from home.

Although the Bible does not tell us how long Moses was traveling, I believe it is safe to say it took him several weeks to make this journey. Along the way, Moses surely crossed paths with other people; however, for some reason, they were not the people Moses chose to stick around with. They were not the kind of people Moses knew he needed to associate with if he was going to change the trajectory of his life going forward.

However, when he came to the home of a godly man named Reuel (later referred to as Jethro), the Bible tells us that Moses decided to remain there. I can just imagine that a portion of Moses' decision had to do with the fact that Jethro had seven daughters. But, I also believe it is important to notice some of the specific words Scripture uses here as Moses makes this decision.

In Exodus 2:16 (CSB) the Bible specifically points out that Jethro was "the priest of Midian." Then, in Exodus 2:21 (CSB), we are told that "Moses agreed to stay with the man." What I believe we see here is that

Moses was thirsting for something that was missing in his life—something he saw in Jethro. Moses was now in the presence of a man who loved God, worshipped God, lived for God, and sought to help others do the same. Consequently, Moses chose to stay with Jethro, and in doing so, he became sensitive to God's voice and plan for his life.

Now, with Moses' example in mind, let me ask you this: Whom are you choosing to surround yourself with today? Are those you choose to associate with the kind of people who lift you up or bring you down? Are you surrounding yourself with individuals who pour godliness into your life, or are they draining, distracting, and distancing you from God's best plan for you?

As you become a part of a church family, you will be surrounded by like-minded people who have a strong desire, not only to read God's Word, but also to grow in their understanding and its application to their lives. One of the most recognizable ways that the Word of God is learned by a church family is through the preaching that occurs during worship services. Every week, all around the world, Christians meet together to, both, lift their voices to God in praise and to hear God speak to them through the reading and teaching of His Word. This ongoing, regular gathering of God's people is what the apostle Paul had in mind when he said, "Some people have given up the habit of meeting for worship, but we must not do that. We should keep on encouraging each other, especially since you know that the day of the Lord's coming is getting closer" (Hebrews 10:25, CEV).

Another way people grow together in their understanding of the Bible is by joining a Bible study group (sometimes called Small Groups, Life Groups, Sunday School, or other similar names). One of the great advantages of being part of a group that regularly meets and studies God's Word together is that it provides each participant with the opportunity to share insights, ask questions, and engage in discussions about the Scripture being studied. This level of interaction is impossible to achieve during the corporate worship setting.

In the Old Testament book of Proverbs, the wisest man to ever live, King Solomon, wrote, "As iron sharpens iron, so one person sharpens another" (Proverbs 27:17, NASB). I want you to consider the imagery Solomon utilizes in this verse. A blade is of no use if it is not straight, strong, and sharp. To shape a piece of metal into what the blacksmith envisions, it must undergo repeated contact with the hammer and the grinding wheel. It is only through continual interaction with these tools that the blade can become straight, strong, and sharp and fulfill the blacksmith's purpose for its existence.

Likewise, one of the most effective ways to lead a life characterized as being straight, strong, and sharp is to consistently engage in the study of God's Word alongside fellow believers. Just as a sword requires contact with both the hammer and the grinding wheel for full and proper development, Christians require ongoing participation in worship services and church-organized Bible study groups to nurture their faith and understanding. Active involvement in these groups and meaningful discussions with fellow believers can offer valuable support and accountability on your spiritual journey.

The Church Is a Place of Function

One of the most common misconceptions about the church is that it is something you show up to and watch—similar to a sporting event, a concert, or a play. The truth, however, is that the church is not a performance you passively observe or a building you simply occupy. The church is a living, breathing organism composed of individuals who have placed their faith in Jesus and are actively engaged in the mission of building God's Kingdom. For the church to be healthy and function as the Lord intends, every member must serve and fulfill their unique role within the body.

Unfortunately, I have had multiple conversations with Christians over the years that followed a similar pattern. Many will say they cannot serve in some specific area of ministry because:

- "I don't know enough."
- "I am too shy."
- "I am not a teacher."
- "I am not good with kids."
- "I am not good with adults."

However, the problem with such thinking lies in the fact that each excuse begins with "I," indicating a reliance on one's own abilities rather than depending upon God. Thankfully, God does not expect us to serve Him based on our own strengths. When God saved us, He equipped us with spiritual gifts through the presence of the Holy Spirit in our lives. This is what Peter was referring to when he wrote, "God has given each of you a gift from His great variety of spiritual gifts. Use them well to serve one another" (1 Peter 4:10, NLT).

Just as the human body is composed of many different parts, so too is the church. Each Christian is endowed with unique spiritual gifts, talents, and personalities by God, enabling us to work together and fulfill His purposes for the church. When parts of the human body fail to function as intended, the body may continue to live, but its capabilities are diminished. Similarly, in a church, if members do not serve in accordance with their God-given design and abilities, the church may persist, but it will suffer, lose its vitality, and struggle to achieve its full potential.

Technology has provided us with a plethora of helpful resources, and if you search the internet, you will find various questionnaires referred to as "spiritual gifts assessments." While some of these tools can be quite useful, I firmly believe the most accurate means of discovering how God has uniquely equipped you for service is to prayerfully choose an area of ministry and start serving. If that place aligns with your God-given gifts and where He wants you to serve, you will experience joy, peace, and fruitful results from your labor. However, if you discern that another area of service might be a better fit for you, do not hesitate to speak with the leader overseeing that specific ministry about making a change.

It is important to recognize that many Christians, myself included, did not initially serve in the roles they currently hold within the church. As individuals become more involved in serving in the church, it is both common and entirely acceptable for them to transition from one area of ministry to another until they discern their most suitable place of service according to God's leading. The benefit of discovering your role in the church through this process, rather than relying solely on a questionnaire, is that God will grow you, use you, and cultivate relationships within your spiritual family as you serve Him by serving others. So, place your trust in God, step out in faith, and embrace the opportunity to serve.

Ponder and Practice

1. **Church as a Family:** Discuss the concept of the church as a family and how this relationship differs from other social groups. Share your experiences of being part of a church family and its impact on your faith journey. Identify ways to deepen these relationships within your church community.

2. **Personal Connection and Engagement in Church:** Discuss ways to prevent church attendance from becoming a mere ritual and ensure it remains a priority for you and your family. Plan specific steps to deepen your connection and engagement during worship and other church activities.

3. **Role of Church in Personal Formation:** Consider the story of Moses, his time with Jethro, and how it potentially influenced his life. Discuss how the church can play a similar role in shaping and guiding individual lives. What experiences have you had in the church that have contributed to your personal growth and spiritual formation?

4. **Active Participation in Biblical Studies and Groups:** Reflect on the value of active participation in Bible studies and small groups. How do these groups enhance your understanding of the Bible? Share your experiences and discuss how they have enriched your faith journey.
5. **Identifying and Serving with Your Spiritual Gifts:** Discuss the importance of active participation in the church, rather than merely observing. Reflect on identifying and using your spiritual gifts. As a practical step, consider the areas of service in your church where you feel drawn to contribute. Plan to engage in one of these areas, even if it is just a trial to discover your gifts and where you can best serve. How will you take the first step toward serving in this way?

Chapter 4

Understanding and Applying God's Word

Your word is a lamp to guide my
feet and a light for my path.

–Psalm 119:105, NLT

MY FAMILY AND I live near Houston, Texas, which means we also live relatively close to two major airports. For some people, this may not be a desirable location, but I enjoy it. You see, my dad worked for American Airlines for forty years, so I have always been fascinated with airplanes and flying. Our proximity to these bustling Houston airports means that there are several pilots and airline employees in our community and our church.

Recently, while talking with one of the pilots in our church, I asked him, "What is one of the first things you do when you sit down in the cockpit to prepare for your flight?" He replied, "I always consult the Quick Reference Handbook, which is basically a condensed version of the flight manual."

So, what is a flight manual? Simply put, it is a book containing the necessary information for pilots to safely operate the aircraft. Before embarking on any trip, all pilots look to this manual, which is designed to ensure that when understood and applied, they and everyone onboard will have a safe and successful journey.

Thankfully, God has provided us with a "flight manual" in the form of the Bible. This sacred text serves as our guide to successfully navigate life on Earth and prepare for eternity. The challenge, though, is that much like a flight manual is of no use to a pilot unless its information is both read and applied, the same is true for Christians regarding the Bible. God's Word must be treated as an integral part of our daily lives.

In the Old Testament book of 2 Kings, we read about a time when God's people neglected the Word of God to such an extent that they literally lost it. The Bible records for us the following:

> *In the eighteenth year of King Josiah, the king sent the court secretary Shaphan son of Azaliah, son of Meshullam, to the Lord's temple, saying, "Go up to the high priest Hilkiah so that he may total up the silver brought into the Lord's temple—the silver the doorkeepers have collected from the people. It is to be given to those doing the work—those who oversee the Lord's temple. They in turn are to give it to the*

workmen in the Lord's temple to repair the damage. They are to give it to the carpenters, builders, and masons to buy timber and quarried stone to repair the temple." –2 Kings 22:3-6, CSB

Here, we witness the neglect and disregard shown toward the maintenance of the Lord's temple. Almost two centuries had passed without any repair work being undertaken. King Josiah, however, was determined to correct this grave oversight and took the initiative by sending his assistant, Shaphan, to discuss the necessary repairs with the high priest. The king was keen on ensuring that the work would be carried out quickly and completely.

During the course of their work, the craftsmen made a remarkable discovery. As the Bible recounts, "The high priest Hilkiah told the court secretary Shaphan, 'I have found the book of the law in the Lord's temple,' and he gave the book to Shaphan, who read it" (2 Kings 22:8, CSB).

The book referenced in this passage might have encompassed the entire Pentateuch, spanning from Genesis to Deuteronomy, or it may have been limited to just the book of Deuteronomy. Either way, I want you to allow this to sink deep into your thinking. God's Word—their Bible—had been lost, forsaken, and hidden away somewhere for a very long period of time, and apparently, no one was very concerned about this. While it may be difficult for us to fathom the actions of God's people in that era, the truth is that the neglect of God's Word continues to persist in modern times as well.

Now, before I go any further, there is something I need to confess. At times, in an attempt to be humorous, I hide my wife's Bible. And although she has other Bibles she can use, this particular one holds a special place in her heart. It is the Bible she takes to church, the one she uses for her Bible studies, and the one she reads during her daily "quiet time." This Bible has notes in the margins, underlined verses, and words that are circled and highlighted. And it is this Bible that I have been known to occasionally hide.

After all these years of marriage, Kim has become accustomed to my strange sense of humor. However, in the early years, she did not find it very amusing. Whenever she would ask me why I did it, I would jokingly tell her that I was just making sure she missed it and was legitimately reading her Bible.

I realize that this book is not about marriage, but as someone who enjoys helping other people, I would like to offer a bit of advice to all the husbands who are reading this. Let me be very clear and say that, today, I do not recommend hiding your wife's Bible. Learn from my mistakes and avoid repeating them. You will thank me later.

All joking aside, we see that approximately 2,600 years ago, the Word of God had been lost and overlooked. God's people and their spiritual leaders had neglected it for so long that they showed no signs of missing it. This highlights a significant deficiency in their dedication to studying and adhering to the Scriptures.

But let me ask you this: What role does God's Word

play in your daily life? As you contemplate your response to that question, I would like to share three beneficial practices that can assist you in experiencing the blessings of God's Word in your life.

#1 – Get God's Word in Your Hands

One of the most important commitments I made several years ago as a young Christian was to pick up my Bible each day. I realized that I needed help, not only with understanding more about who God is, but also with understanding how I should live my life as a husband, father, and follower of Jesus Christ. Now, in full transparency, I must admit that there have been days when I neglected to pick up and read God's Word. And on those occasions, I felt a sense of chaos, as though I were walking through the day in a fog of uncertainty. It was not because negative events automatically unfolded, but rather, I sensed a lack of preparedness to face whatever choices and challenges came my way.

Over the years, I have encountered numerous individuals expressing difficulty in maintaining the daily practice of reading God's Word. When I inquire about their routine, many respond with, "I don't have one. I simply open my Bible and read whatever passage is before me." While this approach might work for some people, I would like to offer a few suggestions that I encourage you to adopt as you endeavor to engage with God's Word daily.

To begin with, having a well-defined plan is crucial.

Establishing a new routine becomes more manageable when guided by a solid plan. The plan I follow involves reading through the Bible in a year. Each morning, I dedicate time to reading from Tyndale House Publishers' *The One Year Bible*. This Bible is divided into 365 daily readings, with portions from the Old Testament and New Testament to be read each day. Through years of personal experience, I have discovered that this plan works exceptionally well for me.

Another reading plan you might want to consider is spending time each day reading through one of the Gospels. For instance, on day one, open your Bible to Mark 1:1 and dedicate five minutes to reading. Then, on day two, simply pick up where you left off. Continue following this plan until you complete that particular book of the Bible.

Once you develop a plan, it is crucial to prioritize daily Bible reading. Every morning when you wake up, you are faced with choices regarding what you will read, whom you will listen to, and where you will seek information and guidance. Unfortunately, many Christians, are quick to turn to various sources of information before turning to God's Word. Text messages, social media posts, and the latest headlines flood in the moment you pick up your phone. While these can be interesting, none of them possess the ability to protect, guide, and bless you like spending the first few minutes of your morning with God in His Word.

I recommend designating a specific place for your daily time in God's Word. For me, that place is a chair in the corner of my home office where I go, most mornings, to read and pray. Setting apart this space serves as a reminder that I am engaging in something truly significant during those moments—I am meeting with, listening to, and speaking to God. Establishing this dedicated place for my daily quiet time also helps eliminate one decision I have to make before getting started. Mornings can be busy, so streamlining the process of getting into God's Word can be incredibly helpful.

Finally, as you hold God's Word in your hands each morning, I encourage you to keep paper nearby for taking notes. Throughout the years, I have discovered that jotting down a few notes about the Scripture I am reading helps me remember it better throughout the day. Additionally, I suggest asking yourself a few simple questions while prayerfully seeking to learn and apply God's Word to your life. Consider questions like:

- "Heavenly Father, based on what I just read, what do You want me to understand about You, and what do You want me to understand about myself?"
- "Heavenly Father, based on what I just read, what do You want me to stop doing, and what do You want me to start doing?"

These reflective questions can deepen your engagement with the Scripture and guide your personal application of its teachings.

As we return to our story in 2 Kings, the Bible tells us the following: "The high priest Hilkiah told the court secretary Shaphan, 'I have found the book of the law in the Lord's temple,' and [the priest] gave the book to Shaphan, who read it. Then the court secretary Shaphan told the king, 'The priest Hilkiah has given me a book,' and Shaphan read it in the presence of the king" (2 Kings 22:8,10, CSB).

From this account, we observe that the king and his assistant now hold God's Word in their hands. It is not some document that is distant—nor is it a collection of writings that they only know of or occasionally hear stories about. Instead, God's Word is near. It is personal. It is touchable. It now rests in their hands as an essential source of wisdom and guidance for their lives.

In the book of Deuteronomy, the Word of God states the following:

> *When he sits on the throne as king, he must copy for himself this body of instruction on a scroll in the presence of the Levitical priests. He must always keep that copy with him and read it daily as long as he lives. That way he will learn to fear the Lord his God by obeying all the terms of these instructions and decrees. This regular reading will prevent him from becoming proud and acting as if he is above his fellow citizens. It will also prevent him from turning away from these commands in the smallest way. And it will ensure that he and his descendants will reign for many generations in Israel.* –Deuteronomy 17:18-20, NLT

This passage emphasizes that Israel's leaders and their descendants would be blessed through their commitment to daily reading of the Word of God. Remarkably, this principle applies to us today as well. Those who make a habit of engaging with God's Word daily will gain an understanding of how to live in ways that invite God's blessings, not only for themselves but also for their families. Taking God's Word into our hands daily enables us to align our lives with His teachings and experience the blessings and transformative power of His guidance.

#2 - Get God's Word in Your Home

If I were to ask you what comes to mind whenever you think of King Josiah, what would you say? Many people would mention the fact that Josiah was only 8 years old when he became king. I want you to think back to what your life was like whenever you were that same age. What kind of a leader do you believe you would have been? Would you have been someone who brought blessings to your people, or would you have been like so many of the Jewish leaders who, not only negatively impacted the nation, but also harmed their own households?

In 2 Kings 22, we learn, not only what kind of king Josiah turned out to be, but we also gain a good understanding of what influenced and directed his decisions. The Bible tells us that "[Josiah] did what was right in the Lord's sight and walked in all the ways of his ancestor David; he did not turn to the right or the left" (2 Kings 22:2, NLT).

While Josiah's ascent to the throne at such a young age is definitely noteworthy, what truly sets him apart is his unwavering devotion to following God's Word. And I believe this deep desire to know and obey God's commands can be traced back to the influence of his ancestor, King David. One of David's notable characteristics, as clearly emphasized in the Bible, is his sincere love for God's Word. In Psalm 119, David writes the following:

> *Oh, how I love your instructions! I think about them all day long. Your commands make me wiser than my enemies, for they are my constant guide. Yes, I have more insight than my teachers, for I am always thinking of your laws. I am even wiser than my elders, for I have kept your commandments.* –Psalm 119:97-100, NLT

Both David and Josiah clearly believed that God's Word was a trustworthy guide for their lives.

In a meeting at church with leaders of our children's ministry, we discussed the significance of encouraging families to engage in studying God's Word in their homes. During our conversation, we reviewed a survey conducted by Lifeway Research. The survey's primary focus, as stated by the executive director of Lifeway Research, Scott McConnell, was "to know what parenting practices pay off over the long haul when it comes to [children's] spiritual health."[11]

---

[11] Bob Smietana, "Young Bible Readers More Likely to Be Faithful Adults, Study Finds," LifeWay Research, accessed October 17, 2017, https://lifewayresearch.com/2017/10/17/young-bible-readers-more-likely-to-be-faithful-adults-study-finds/.

McConnell stated that their research revealed a significant finding. The most reliable predictor of a spiritually healthy young adult is the regular reading of the Bible in their childhood home. This factor held more influence than listening to Christian music, participating in mission trips, or receiving instructions on what they should do. Lifeway's research concluded that the consistent reading of God's Word, both with children and by children, had a substantial impact on their spiritual development in their later years as young adults.

This is why I urge every mom and dad to see themselves as God sees them. If you are a parent, your greatest role in this world is not that of a prosperous businessman or businesswoman. Instead, your highest calling and most significant responsibility is to be the primary disciple-maker in your home, particularly with your children. Moms and dads, we possess the greatest capacity to shape our children's lives for Jesus, and this responsibility cannot be delegated to anyone else, not even to your church.

I realize that, for many of us, our children no longer reside at home. However, just because they have grown up and moved out of the house does not make it impossible for us to impact them for Christ. It may require some creativity, but I encourage you to ask yourself, "What actions can I take today to bless and influence my adult children and grandchildren to know and follow God's Word?"

Many of you are familiar with the life and ministry of the late evangelist Billy Graham. His wife, Ruth, is quoted as saying, "If our children have the background of a godly, happy home and this unshakable faith that the Bible is indeed the Word of God, they will have a foundation that the forces of Hell cannot shake."[12]

Moms and dads, does that description match the environment you are creating in your home? If not, it can become a reality. However, it requires taking action and getting started today.

The Word of God instructs us, "You must commit yourselves wholeheartedly to [God's] commands… Repeat [God's Word] again and again to your children. Talk about [God's Word] when you are at home and when you are on the road, when you are going to bed and when you are getting up" (Deuteronomy 6:6-7, NLT).

As a pastor, I am deeply grateful for the unwavering dedication of our volunteers and staff to faithfully teach children about Jesus every time they are on our campus. The knowledge and commitment of these Christ followers is truly commendable. However, as remarkable as they and their efforts may be, an even better plan for impacting children exists! This plan involves moms and dads committing themselves to getting God's Word into their homes and teaching their children to cherish and obey it.

---

[12] Billy Graham, *Peace with God: The Secret of Happiness* (Nashville: Harper Collins Publishers, 1953, 1984), 21.

#3 – Get God's Word into Your Heart

As you continue reading King Josiah's story, 2 Kings 23 reveals that the king had everyone, both young and old, gather to meet with him outside of the Lord's temple. Once the people were all assembled, Josiah proceeded to do the following:

> *He read in their hearing all the words of the book of the covenant that had been found in the Lord's temple. Next, the king... made a covenant in the Lord's presence to follow the Lord and to keep his commands, his decrees, and his statutes with all his heart and with all his soul in order to carry out the words of this covenant that were written in this book; all the people agreed to the covenant.* –2 Kings 23:2-3, CSB

In this passage, we see that it is not enough for us just to read the Bible. We actually have to apply it. God's Word has to move from something only in our hands and make its way into our hearts. This transformation occurred in Josiah's time among God's people. In fact, if you read the rest of 2 Kings 23, you will encounter a long list of actions undertaken by Josiah, his leaders, and the people. They began removing all sinful elements from their lives and from the land that had hindered them from experiencing God's power and blessings.

After the Word of God went to work on the people's hearts, the people went to work for God. This is because what we cherish and hold dear in our hearts profoundly influences our conduct. If we genuinely love Jesus Christ and treasure God's Word, it will manifest in our actions and be evident not only to God but also to everyone around us through the way we live.

With this understanding in mind, I want you to do something. I want you to reflect on the past six to twelve months of your life. As you look back, what do you see? Did you allow things to enter your hands, your home, and your heart that influenced you more toward God or more toward the world? If you find yourself saying, "I don't know," then consider it from this perspective: How would the people closest to you answer that question about you? What would they say filled your hands, your home, and your heart? Was it the increasing presence of God or an increasing influence of the world?

Not long ago, I was reading *God In My Corner* by George Foreman. In this book, the former heavyweight boxing champion wrote, "In 1974, before I went to Manilla to fight Muhammad Ali, a friend gave me a Bible to take along on my trip."[13] Foreman said this friend instructed him to keep the Bible with him for good luck. The boxer admitted to being a man who was always looking for luck, so he did as his friend suggested and carried the Bible with him on his trip. Foreman said, "I had lucky pennies and good luck charms, so now I added the 'lucky' Bible to my collection of superstitious items."[14]

However, if you are familiar with Foreman's career,

---

[13] George Foreman and Ken Abraham, *God In My Corner* (Nashville: Thomas Nelson, 2007), 91.

[14] Ibid.

you know that he was defeated by Ali. After experiencing that loss, Foreman threw the Bible away without ever opening it. He later admitted that he thought he would get power simply from owning it. However, what Foreman eventually discovered was that he not only needed God's Word in his hands but he also needed it in his heart.

So, where is it for you? Where is God's Word in relation to your life? If you want to experience God and His incredible plan, you can, but you must get God's Word in your hands. You must get God's Word in your home. And you must get God's Word in your heart.

Ponder and Practice

1. **Integrating God's Word into Daily Life:** Reflect on how you currently integrate the Bible into your daily routine. Discuss the benefits and challenges you face in maintaining this practice. As a practical step, consider adopting a specific Bible reading plan (like *The One Year Bible* or reading one chapter of a Gospel daily) and commit to following it for a set period of time. How will this structured approach impact your engagement with Scripture?
2. **God's Word in the Home:** Considering the influence of God's Word in shaping young lives, discuss the importance of incorporating the Bible into family life. Share ideas on how to make Bible reading and discussion a regular part of family interactions. For those with children at home, what specific steps can you take to include Scripture reading in your family routines? For those without children at home, how can you encourage and support Bible engagement in your extended family or community?
3. **Applying Scripture to Personal Life:** Reflect on King Josiah's response to hearing God's Word: a

commitment to apply it wholeheartedly. Discuss how you can move from simply reading the Bible to actively applying its teachings in your daily life. What recent passage or verse has particularly struck you, and what practical changes can you make to align your life more closely with its message?

4. **Bible Engagement and Heart Transformation:** Examine the concept of the Bible transforming not just our minds, but also our hearts. Share a personal experience where reading and reflecting on God's Word led to a significant change in your attitude, behavior, or decisions. How can you cultivate a habit of allowing Scripture to continually work on your heart?
5. **Self-Reflection and Action Plan for Spiritual Growth:** Reflect on what has filled your hands, home, and heart in the past six to twelve months. How can this guide you to make more God-centered choices? Identify one area of your life (e.g., entertainment, relationships, work) needing alignment with God's Word. Develop a plan to address this, incorporating specific Scriptures for guidance.

Chapter 5

Cultivating a Prayerful Life

Call to me and I will answer you and tell you great and incomprehensible things you do not know.

–Jeremiah 33:3, CSB

AS YOU READ through the Bible, one of the amazing lessons you will learn is that God is conversational. He desires to both be heard *and* to hear people speaking to Him. And yet, one of the most underutilized and misunderstood aspects of the Christian life has to be the discipline of prayer.

So, what is prayer? In her insightful book on the topic, Rosalind Rinker defines prayer as "the expression of the human heart in conversation with God."[15] In other words, prayer involves a Christian engaging in

---

[15] Rosalind Rinker, *Prayer: Conversing With God* (Grand Rapids: Zondervan Publishing House, 1959), 23.

a heart-to-heart dialogue with God. I understand that, for some, the idea of conversing with God might seem unusual. However, it is worth noting that the same God who communicated with people like Noah, Moses, and David throughout the Bible remains unchanged today. God has consistently shown His desire to communicate with His people daily.

But before we go any further, here is a question I would like to ask you: Do you consider yourself to be a good listener? You may think so, but what if I asked your spouse? Or, better yet, what if I asked your dog? I would never recommend asking a cat anything, because cats never tell the truth. Dogs, however, are honest and trustworthy animals. So, what would your dog have to say? Are you a good listener?

While it is very important for us to speak freely whenever we are praying, I also believe that, many times, we tend to over-talk. What do I mean by that? Well, so many times we pray for God to guide us or to give us wisdom, but do we ever just sit in silence and wait for Him to lead us? Are we always telling God what we think He should do, or do we ever give Him the opportunity to shape our thoughts, desires, and understanding?

In Psalm 27, David wrote, "Hear me as I pray, O Lord. Be merciful and answer me! My heart has heard you say, 'Come and talk with me.' And my heart responds, 'Lord, I am coming'" (Psalm 27:7-8, NLT).

Then, later on, in the midst of a very difficult time, David wrote, "I wait quietly before God, for my victory comes from him. Let all that I am wait quietly before God, for my hope is in him" (Psalm 62:1, 5, NLT).

Verses such as these are the reason I say prayer is a conversation, and the most intimate and effective kind of communication is one that goes both ways. In other words, not only do I have input into the conversation, but I also look to receive input from the other person. So, if prayer involves both speaking to God and hearing from Him, then how do we do it? How do we communicate with God?

Prioritize Time with God Daily

The primary reason why a significant number of Christians do not regularly receive guidance from God is that we often fail to genuinely seek His input and direction. So many believers neglect to make prayer a daily priority and subsequently become frustrated with what they perceive as His lack of concern and communication. However, I am convinced that if we could perceive what is on God's heart when He sees us rushing out the door to begin our day without including Him, we would hear Him saying, "Where are you heading in such a hurry? Child of Mine, if you would just slow down and prioritize spending time with Me, I would give you the wisdom and assistance you need. I will show you the best path—My blessed path—for your life."

Please do not think that my aim is to get everyone to do exactly what I do and the way I do it. That is not my intention at all. However, based on my personal experience and what I have learned from the Bible, I do believe that the best time to regularly "meet" with God is at the beginning of every day. This has been my routine for many years, and it has proven to be the most effective approach for me.

I have heard it said that the first hour of the day is like the rudder of a ship. It is going to determine where you end up at the end of the day. There might be someone reading this and thinking, "Did you say morning? I'm not really a morning person." I understand that sentiment as many people feel the same way. However, the issue is not really whether or not I am a morning person or a night person. The issue is if I am the kind of person who wants to hear from God or not. In other words, how serious am I about knowing God better and understanding God's will? Because, if I sincerely want to know God better, then I will be willing to adjust my schedule and habits so that I can spend time with Him.

As you read through the Old Testament, you see that David cried out to God in prayer, saying, "Let me hear of Your unfailing love to me in the morning. For I am trusting You. Show me where to walk for I have come to You in prayer" (Psalm 143:8, NLT). Clearly, David saw prayer as an opportunity to receive the guidance he desperately needed at the beginning of each new day.

Then, when you turn to the New Testament and look specifically at the example of Jesus, you see that He, too, began His days by spending time in prayer. In the Gospel of Mark, we read: "Very early in the morning, while it was still dark, [Jesus] got up, went out, and made his way to a deserted place; and there he was praying" (Mark 1:35, CSB). Some might be tempted to say, "Oh, sure! It was easy for Jesus to get up before daybreak and pray. He was the Son of God. If I had God's power like Jesus did, I would be able to get up early and pray also." However, the incredible truth is that Jesus was not only fully God but He was also fully man. And as the God/Man, Jesus faced the same issues you and I encounter daily: fatigue, the demands of others, the struggles of everyday life, and more. Nevertheless, Jesus recognized the profound significance of engaging in dialogue with His Heavenly Father, a realization that prompted Him to deliberately rise early and begin each new day in prayer.

In John 10:27 (NLT), Jesus said, "My sheep listen to my voice; I know them, and they follow me." Now, you may not know this about sheep, but they are not very intelligent animals. However, sheep learn to recognize the voice of their shepherd who provides for them and protects them because they are with him daily. Similarly, if you commit to dedicating time to God each morning, you will also cultivate the ability to discern the voice of your Shepherd. Through this daily routine, you will experience spiritual growth and obtain the guidance necessary to successfully navigate each day of your life.

Learn to Say Yes Even Before God Speaks

One of the primary obstacles to spiritual growth in the Christian life is an individual's lack of obedience. Unfortunately, there are moments when we condition our obedience on the nature of God's instructions. For instance, in prayer, we might say, "God, please reveal Your will for me, and I will do it." However, simultaneously, we might think, "God, I am willing to obey, but only if it does not require sacrifice or significant changes in my life." This mindset does not reflect the attitude and commitment of someone who has genuinely made Jesus their Lord. Conditional obedience often leads to a hardening of the heart, making it more and more difficult to comprehend God's will.

Contrast this with the attitude of a person earnestly desiring to understand God's will. This believer is entirely open and surrendered to the Lordship and authority of Jesus. The prevailing attitude and prayer of such an individual is: "Yes, Lord. Just tell me what You want me to do. I will show up with palms up ready to receive and do whatever assignment You place in my hands."

In the book of Isaiah, God's prophet shared a sobering announcement regarding the impact of sin on a person's life. Isaiah said to God's people: "It's your sins that have cut you off from God. Because of your sins, he has turned away and will not listen anymore" (Isaiah 59:2, NLT).

Have you ever experienced a clogged drain in your

sink? If you ignore the problem, you know that you will eventually end up with a mess, and potentially, quite an expensive one. However, if you get rid of whatever is clogging the line as soon as you become aware of it, then everything will work like it is designed to, and the water will once again flow freely.

That is the way it is with sin. If you hold on to some type of sin in your life, then the line of communication between God and you will become clogged, and you need to deal with it—quickly and completely. The biblical way to do this is through prayer. Confess your sin to God and ask for His forgiveness. Then, after confessing it to God, turn your back on that sinful attitude or action and say, "God, with Your help, I will go in a different direction—the direction that You alone say I am to go."

In the Old Testament, we read the following message from God in the book of Isaiah: "'My thoughts are nothing like your thoughts,' says the LORD. 'And my ways are far beyond anything you could imagine. For just as the heavens are higher than the earth, so my ways are higher than your ways and my thoughts higher than your thoughts'" (Isaiah 55:8-9, NLT).

God knows what is best for you, and He will be faithful to always lead you on the right path. Therefore, do not hesitate to obey. Always be willing to say "yes" to God even before you hear His directions.

A missionary to Africa shared the story of native converts to Christianity in his area. They were dedicated to God and consistent in their private devotions. Each believer had a designated spot in the wooded, grassy area surrounding their village where they poured out their hearts to God in prayer. Over time, these paths became well-worn.

Consequently, if any believer began to neglect their prayer time, it became evident to the entire community. With love and humility, fellow believers would approach the one falling behind and gently say, "Friend, there's grass on your path."[16] This simple phrase served as a reminder that their connection with God was showing signs of neglect.

In the days ahead, I encourage you to ask yourself the following questions: What does the path to where I meet with God in prayer look like? Is it well-worn, or have I been neglecting time with God? Has the path to my prayer place become overgrown with weeds?

Pray the Way Jesus Taught Us to Pray

In Luke 11, the Bible chronicles a time when Jesus was praying. Now, understand that there was nothing unusual about Jesus praying. Prayer was something He did frequently. However, on this occasion, instead of going off in solitude, we discover that Jesus was praying in close proximity to His disciples. Then, as Jesus concluded praying, one of His disciples approached Him

---

[16] RWD, "Grass On Your Path," *Our Daily Bread*, November 18, 1996.

and said, "Lord, teach us to pray" (Luke 11:1, NLT). In response, Jesus shared those very familiar words we refer to as The Lord's Prayer.

Now, before I go any further, allow me to clarify something very important. The words of this prayer were not given by Jesus to be recited like some special incantation. Instead, Jesus' intention was for these words to serve as a model or a framework for His followers whenever we engage in praying.

Picking up the conversation in Matthew 6, Jesus answered His disciple by saying this:

> *"Pray, then, in this way:*
> *'Our Father, who is in heaven,*
> *Hallowed be Your name.*
> *Your kingdom come.*
> *Your will be done,*
> *On earth as it is in heaven.*
> *'Give us this day our daily bread.*
> *'And forgive us our debts, as we also*
> *have forgiven our debtors.*
> *'And do not lead us into temptation,*
> *but deliver us from evil.'"*
>
> –*Matthew 6:9-13, NASB*

While I believe it is encouraging and helpful for all of us to memorize these specific words, it is even more important for us to understand what Jesus wanted His people to do as a result of what He said. In other words—what Jesus said needs to shape the way we pray. And for me,

I have found the acrostic ACTS to be a very helpful framework for praying. Consider the following:

A–Adoration

As Jesus begins this prayer, His focus, first and foremost, is on worshipping God and praising Him. Instead of beginning with a list of wants and wishes, Jesus clearly begins His model prayer by expressing His love and reverence for the Creator and Ruler of all—God the Father.

C–Confession

Soon after adoration, Jesus shows us that confession is an integral part of prayer. Now, do not misunderstand me. I am not suggesting that Jesus was admitting some personal sin of His own. Jesus never sinned. However, unlike Jesus, we are prone to wrongdoing. Therefore, we need to approach God promptly upon recognizing any transgression, confessing our sin and seeking His forgiveness.

T–Thanksgiving

Next, Jesus shows us the importance of giving thanks to God. I have heard it said that "Without gratitude, we become arrogant and self-centered. We begin to believe that we have achieved everything on our own."[17] However, when we give thanks to God, we humbly

---

[17] "Why Is Giving Thanks To God Important?" Got Questions Ministries, accessed June 11, 2022, https://www.gotquestions.org/giving-thanks-to-God.html

declare our gratitude and our dependence upon the Giver of all good gifts.

S–Supplication

According to the dictionary, supplication is "the act of asking a god or someone who is in a position of power for something in a humble way."[18] In His model prayer, Jesus not only lets us know that it is okay for us to make requests of God, but He actually encourages us to do so regularly. Jesus used words like "give us this day" and "daily" to show us that communication with God was to be frequent and ongoing. He is our loving Heavenly Father, and He is both willing and able to help us and the people we are praying for with our needs.

Just as good communication is vital in any marriage, friendship, or work environment, so it is in our relationship with God. For that most important of our relationships to be healthy and growing as God intends, there has to be a commitment on our part to sincere and frequent prayer. And, when we do, we will discover the joy and the blessing it is to both speak to and hear from our Heavenly Father each day.

---

[18] "Supplication," *Cambridge Dictionary*, s.v., accessed May 12, 2021, https://dictionary.cambridge.org/us/dictionary/english/supplication.

Ponder and Practice

1. **Understanding and Practicing Prayer:** Reflect on your current understanding and practice of prayer. How do you define prayer, and what does it mean to you to have a conversation with God? Share personal experiences where prayer has been particularly meaningful or challenging. As a practical step, try incorporating a new aspect of prayer into your routine, such as silence, writing out your prayer, or creating a prayer journal logging asked and answered prayers.
2. **Prioritizing Daily Prayer:** Discuss the importance of making prayer a daily priority. What obstacles do you face in maintaining a consistent prayer routine, and how can you address them? Commit to a specific time and place for daily prayer over the next month and share your plan with a fellow believer for support.
3. **Openness and Obedience in Prayer:** Consider the concept of saying "yes" to God before knowing His instructions. How does this attitude affect your approach to prayer and your readiness to follow God's guidance? During your next prayer

time, consciously surrender your own desires and plans, opening yourself to whatever God may direct.

4. **Evaluating the "Path" to Your Prayer Life:** Reflect on the metaphor of the "grass on your path" regarding prayer. Evaluate the current state of your prayer life: is the path well-worn or overgrown? Identify one action you can take to revitalize your prayer routine, such as joining a prayer group, setting reminders, or incorporating prayer into daily activities like commuting.
5. **Using The Lord's Prayer as a Framework:** Explore how The Lord's Prayer can serve as an outline for your own prayers. Discuss each element of the ACTS acrostic (Adoration, Confession, Thanksgiving, Supplication) and how it can enhance your prayer life. Over the next week, structure your prayers using this model, focusing on each aspect for a day or two, and observe any changes in your prayer life and spiritual growth.

Chapter 6

The Power of Worship in Your Life

Love the LORD your God with all your heart,
with all your soul, and with all your strength.

–Deuteronomy 6:5, CSB

ONE DAY, WHILE doing some reading, I came across a headline that caught my attention. At the top of this article were the words: "What You Can't See Can Hurt You."[19] Now, I don't know about you, but when I see words like that, you have my attention. So, I started reading and found that this article was talking about empty spaces that can form under your house or your driveway in places you cannot see.

---

[19] "What You Can't See, Can Hurt You," Concrete Raising Systems, accessed October 19, 2021, https://www.liftyourconcrete.com/what-you-cant-see-can-hurt-you/.

Thankfully, I have never had to deal with this type of problem in any of the homes we have owned. However, others know firsthand just how big of a problem this can be. They are well aware of the fact that their house can be missing a lot of things and still be okay, but if they are missing the soil under your foundation, then they are going to have a major problem.

As I continued reading this article, I started thinking about the Christian life. I wondered what would cause a Christian to say, "If this one thing is missing from my life, I am going to have problems." While there are several significant facets to consider, it strikes me that worship stands out as a crucial component that must be present. Its absence can deeply affect a believer's spiritual well-being and relationship with God.

Why do I say that?

Well, one day, an expert in religious law approached Jesus and asked Him, "Teacher, which command in the law is the greatest?" (Matthew 22:36, CSB). Jesus answered this man by saying, "Love the Lord your God with all your heart, with all your soul, and with all your mind. This is the greatest and most important command" (Matthew 22:37-38, CSB).

This commandment captures the core of our Christian journey. It is a directive that goes beyond mere feelings or ritualistic actions. It is a call to an all-encompassing commitment to God, and central to this commitment to loving God is worship. Worship is not something to be done only on Sunday mornings. True worship is a dynamic expression of our love for God. It is a way to honor, adore, and express our devotion to Him, permeating every aspect of our lives.

The Priority of Worship

In Acts 16, we read about Paul and his companions as they were ministering in the city of Philippi. As these men were walking to a prayer gathering, Paul encountered a slave girl who made money for her masters by purportedly predicting people's futures. As Paul continued walking, she followed along making comments about him. Eventually, Paul turned toward the young woman and commanded the demon controlling her to depart.

As you can well imagine, this turn of events did not sit well with her masters. They recognized that Paul's actions had terminated a continuous source of their income. Consequently, they seized both Paul and Silas and made them appear before the city authorities. In this setting, the young woman's masters proceeded to level a variety of false accusations against both Paul and Silas.

Then, in Acts 16:22-25 (CSB), we read the following:

> *The crowd joined in the attack against them, and the chief magistrates stripped off their clothes and ordered them to be beaten with rods. After they had severely flogged them, they threw them in jail, ordering the jailer to guard them carefully. Receiving such an order, he put them into the inner prison and secured their feet in the stocks.*

> *About midnight Paul and Silas were praying and singing hymns to God, and the prisoners were listening to them.*

Now that you have read the preceding passage, I have a question: How would you respond if someone treated you harshly due to your Christian faith? Would your response be one of worry or worship? The truth is that most Christians in America will likely never endure persecution to the extent that Paul did. Consequently, it is reasonable to assume that most believers are not overly concerned about such a possibility.

But what will be your response when the next major problem arises in your life, such as receiving distressing news or witnessing a loved one in pain? How will you react? Will you succumb to worry, or will you choose to worship? I pose these questions because I have come to understand this about worrying: Whenever we engage in worry, our focus shifts from God to ourselves. As a result, we concentrate all our time, thoughts, and energy on us—the ones who do the struggling—rather than on Jesus—the One who does the saving—and this is neither healthy nor helpful.

Not long ago, I came across an illustration that pastor Tony Evans shared. Evans wrote:

> *The sun is a light twenty-four hours a day, seven days a week. All year long, all decade long, all century long, the sun just keeps on shining. The problem, however, is that the earth gets dark. How can there be all that light and the earth still gets dark? The earth gets dark*

because the earth is spinning on its axis. Therefore, the side that faces the sun gets light, and the side that is facing away [lives in darkness].

If there is darkness in your life, it's not because God, the Father of Lights, is turning; it's because you are turning. He is the Father of Lights and in Him there is no shadow. There is no darkness in Him. Because God is faithful, He's consistent. Just like the sun, He is always shining, and in His light, there is no shifting or moving shadow. We just have to make sure we are always turning toward Him.[20]

I am not suggesting that worshipping God will keep you from having problems. We live in a world that has been marred and scarred by sin, and problems will exist as long as we exist on this planet. What I am saying, though, is that Paul knew God loved him and that God could see him where he was—locked up and in chains in a prison. Paul also knew he could either worry about his condition or engage in worshipping the God who could help him, and that is what Paul and Silas chose to do. They chose to worship the One who could lift their spirits, heal their wounds, and even set them free—if that's what God chose to do.

So, how much of a priority is worshipping God for you? Is it something you do only if it is convenient and when everything is good? Or is worshipping God

---

[20] Tony Evans, *Tony Evans' Book of Illustrations: Stories, Quotes, and Anecdotes From More Than 30 Years of Preaching and Public Speaking* (Chicago: Moody Publishers, 2009), 128.

a priority—something you do every day regardless of what you are experiencing? Our worship does nothing to change or add to God. However, He deserves it, and it truly is an uplifting blessing to us.

The Practice of Worship

Looking back at Paul and Silas in prison, the Bible tells us this: "About midnight Paul and Silas were praying and singing hymns to God, and the prisoners were listening to them" (Acts 16:25, CSB). In this single setting, we observe two distinctly different responses. One group, consisting only of Paul and Silas, worshipped. The other group, which included all the other prisoners, only listened. Both groups experienced similar conditions and had the same opportunity, but only one group chose to worship.

With this in mind, the question I want you to consider, then, is this: Who was responsible for getting Paul and Silas to worship? Was it:

A. The prison guard's responsibility
B. The people in the next cell's responsibility
C. The prison praise band's responsibility
D. None of the above

The correct answer is "D—None of the above." This is because Paul and Silas were responsible for who and when they worshipped.

Now, with that understanding in mind, let me ask

you this: Who is responsible for getting you and me to worship? Is it:

- **A.** The responsibility of your pastor
- **B.** The responsibility of your spouse
- **C.** The responsibility of the worship leader and the praise band
- **D.** None of the above

Once again, the correct answer is "D—None of the above." Now, I want to be very clear. I am thankful to God for the preachers, singers, and musicians who step out in front of congregations Sunday after Sunday seeking to lead people like you and me to worship. However, no matter how much they preach, perform, or pray, the decision and the responsibility to dedicate my heart, mind, and voice to Jesus through worship ultimately rests with me.

Have you ever walked out of a church service and said to someone, "I didn't get anything out of that worship service today. They didn't sing the songs I like, there were too many guitars, and that guy who was preaching spoke way too long"? Have you ever thought or actually said that? If so, then let me ask you this: Have you ever stopped and wondered, "What did God get out of my effort to worship Him today? Did I genuinely praise Him and thank Him? Did I lift my voice to the One who gave me a voice and so much more? Did I actually worship Him as Jesus said to worship God—'with all [my] heart, with all [my] soul, with all [my] mind, and with all [my] strength'" (Mark 12:30, CSB)?

The truth is that no one can *make* you worship in that way. Genuine worship—the kind that honors God and that God will accept—is a choice that every Christian has to make.

And just to be very transparent with you, I will admit that there are times when I walk into the church building and do not *feel* like worshipping. Sometimes, my mind, my body, or some difficult information I just received is working against me and trying to prevent me from worshipping. Does that exempt me from the need to worship—just because I do not necessarily feel like it? Absolutely not!

Think about it like this: The next time your children do something that you do not approve of, try asking them to tell you why they did not do the right thing. And if your child says, "I just didn't feel like it," what will be your response? Are you going to say, "Oh, no problem. You didn't feel like doing the right thing so that makes it okay"? I can just imagine that your response will be completely different. My guess is that you will say something like, "Do the right thing *first* and let your feelings catch up later."

I am sure Paul and Silas were not feeling their best as they sat in chains within a prison cell, having just suffered a public beating. However, despite their feelings and their incredibly difficult circumstances, they made the choice to worship God. And as we are about to see, when they focused their attention on God, He revealed His power to them.

The Product of Worship

Picking up in Acts 16:26, the Bible tells us that after Paul and Silas worshipped, the following took place:

> *Suddenly there was such a violent earthquake that the foundations of the jail were shaken, and immediately all the doors were opened, and everyone's chains came loose. When the jailer woke up and saw the doors of the prison standing open, he drew his sword and was going to kill himself, since he thought the prisoners had escaped.*
>
> *But Paul called out in a loud voice, "Don't harm yourself, because we're all here!"*
>
> *The jailer called for lights, rushed in, and fell down trembling before Paul and Silas. He escorted them out and said, "Sirs, what must I do to be saved?"*
>
> *They said, "Believe in the Lord Jesus, and you will be saved—you and your household." And they spoke the word of the Lord to him along with everyone in his house. He took them the same hour of the night and washed their wounds. Right away he and all his family were baptized. He brought them into his house, set a meal before them, and rejoiced because he had come to believe in God with his entire household.* – Acts 16:26-34, CSB

Here, the Bible shows us that when Paul and Silas worshipped, the power of God was made known to these men and to all of the people around them. As they lifted their voices in worship, singing songs and proclaiming

God's message, the Bible tells us that the foundation of the jail began to shake. And as God shook things up, the chains fell off, and the doors of the prison cells flew open.

Now, let me ask you a question. Had you been standing there watching all of this take place, what would you have anticipated seeing these two men doing after being miraculously set free? Would you have expected to see them staying or fleeing? I would have expected to see them running as far and as fast as they could. But they didn't. Instead, what we witness is a sense of peace in both Paul and Silas. Regardless of the chaos that was going on around them, they were experiencing God's peace and His power because they prioritized and practiced worship.

I believe one of the reasons so many Christians do not have more peace or see more of God's power and provision is because they have started worshipping some*thing* or some*one* other than God. They have started worshipping that which was created instead of worshipping the Creator. And God makes it very clear that He will not settle for second place in a believer's heart.

In Exodus 34:14 (NLT), God said this: "You must worship no other gods, for the LORD, whose very name is Jealous, is a God who is jealous about his relationship with you."

But how can we evaluate who or what we are actually worshipping? In his book, titled *The Air I Breathe: Worship as a Way of Life*, Louie Giglio wrote:

> *It's easy. You simply follow the trail of your time, your affection, your energy, your money, and your loyalty. At the end of that trail you'll find a throne; and whatever, or whomever, is on that throne is what's of highest value to you. On that throne is what you worship.*
>
> *Sure, not too many of us walk around saying, "I worship my stuff. I worship my X-Box. I worship this pleasure. I worship her. I worship my body. I worship me!"*
>
> *But the trail never lies. We may say we value this thing or that thing more than any other, but the volume of our actions speaks louder than our words.*
>
> *In the end, our worship is more about what we do than what we say.*[21]

So, who or what is sitting on the throne of your heart? Does the occupant of that throne have the power to give you lasting peace? And can the one who rules your heart set you free from whatever seeks to harm and hinder you?

Jesus said, "The thief comes only to steal and kill and destroy. I have come that [you] may have life, and have it in all its fullness" (John 10:10, BSB).

No one loves you like Jesus loves you. No *thing* can bless you like Jesus can bless you. He alone is Lord. He alone is worthy of our worship, today.

---

[21] Louie Giglio, *The Air I Breathe: Worship as a Way of Life* (Colorado Springs: Multnomah, 2017), 3.

Ponder and Practice

1. **The Essence of Worship in Daily Life:** What does worship mean to you? Reflect on how worship is integrated into your daily life outside of a church setting. Share examples of how worship has impacted your relationship with God. As a practical step, identify one way to incorporate worship into your daily routine, such as through music, prayer, or reading Scripture, and commit to this practice for a specific period of time.
2. **Worship in Difficult Circumstances:** Considering the story of Paul and Silas in prison, discuss how you can maintain a spirit of worship during challenging times in your own life. What are the barriers to worshiping in difficult circumstances, and how can you overcome them? As a practical application, the next time you face a trial or a challenging situation, make a conscious effort to turn to worship as your first response and note the changes in your perspective.
3. **Personal Responsibility for Worship:** Examine the concept that each individual is responsible for their own worship. How does this affect your

approach to worship, both publicly and privately? Evaluate your current attitude toward worship and identify one area where you can take greater personal responsibility, such as engaging more actively in church services or setting aside time for personal worship at home.

4. **The Impact of Worship:** Discuss the connection between worship and experiencing God's peace and power. Share personal experiences where worship led to a deeper sense of peace or a greater awareness of God's power and presence in your life. As a practical application, commit to a period of focused worship in a private setting.
5. **Evaluating What You Truly Worship:** Reflect on Louie Giglio's statement about following the trail of your time, affection, energy, money, and loyalty to determine what you truly worship. Take an honest assessment of where these resources are primarily directed in your life. What does this reveal about your true objects of worship? Choose one or more areas where you can redirect more of these resources toward God and create a strategy for this change.

Chapter 7
Joyful Stewardship and Preparedness

Now, a person who is put in charge
as a manager must be faithful.

–1 Corinthians 4:2, NLT

I HAVE BEEN a pastor for more than 27 years, and right now and right here, I am going to make a confession. Are you ready for this? Here it goes. I do not like to talk about money. Somewhere deep down in my memory are the voices I have heard in the past that said, "Preachers only want your money." While I cannot speak for all preachers, I can definitely speak for myself and say this preacher is not interested in your finances. I am, however, very interested in growing your faith. And I have learned over time that my faith impacts my finances and that my finances impact my faith. However, this is nothing new.

Consider the story of the boy who shared his lunch with Jesus. In John 6, the Bible tells us about a boy who went out, one day, to hear Jesus as He was teaching. And as this boy's heart affected what he held in his hands, God used him to make a positive impact on thousands of people's lives. Beginning in verse 1 of John 6, the Word of God says this:

> *Jesus crossed the Sea of Galilee (or Tiberias). A huge crowd was following him, seeing the signs he performed by healing the sick. Jesus went up a mountain and sat with his disciples. The Passover was near. Jesus looked up, noticed a huge crowd, and asked Philip, "Where will we buy bread so these people can eat?" He knew what he was going to do, but he asked to test Philip.* –John 6:1-6, CSB

The setting is somewhere near the city of Bethsaida which is located on the northern edge of the Sea of Galilee. As our story commences, we find Jesus sitting on a hillside, surrounded by His disciples. What initially began as a time for rest and instruction quickly evolved into an opportunity for Jesus to teach and minister to a multitude of people in need.

As the day was coming to an end, Jesus turned toward Philip, one of His disciples, and asked, "Where can we buy enough bread to feed all these people before we send them to their homes?"

At that moment, I can just imagine Philip thinking to himself, "Oh, great! Why did I choose the front row in class today? I had no idea there was going to be a quiz."

From a practical standpoint, this questioning of Philip likely seemed reasonable to the onlookers. After all, Philip was one of three disciples who had spent their formative years in this region. This meant that if anyone was going to know where to find a great restaurant, a convenience store, or a really good drive-thru burger joint, it would probably be Philip. However, instead of offering any practical advice or demonstrating a little faith, Philip responded with doubt: "Two hundred denarii wouldn't suffice to give even a small portion to each one" (John 6:7, CSB).

Now, think about what took place. Philip was sitting next to the Son of God. He had seen Jesus turn water into wine, heal the sick, make the lame walk, and even raise a dead girl back to life. Yet, in that crucial moment, Philip became preoccupied with his own limited resources and abilities. This disciple, who had been a witness to numerous miracles, chose a mindset of self-reliance instead of trusting in the God of limitless power. As a result, Philip's response to Jesus was one of doubt and defeat, saying, "This cannot be done."

While every believer should know and understand the details of this narrative, it is crucial not to view it merely as a history lesson. We need to contextualize this story in our present day, recognizing that Jesus' questioning of Philip is also relevant to us.

I believe it's as though Jesus continues to ask, "Hey, Dale (insert your name here)! Do you see what I see? Do you notice the needs and opportunities in your community, your workplace, and the world? I know what I want to do. I know what I am capable of doing, but I want to know if you are with Me. I want to know if you are willing to trust Me, join Me, and work with Me as a part of My solution."

Sadly, many Christians frequently feel overwhelmed and discouraged when they observe the immense needs of this world. They look around and think, "The need is so great, and I am so small." This mindset often leads to doubting God's ability to work through them, which, in turn, results in a reluctance to act. In moments like these, our limited faith can unintentionally limit the work of God through us.

While I understand that God can accomplish His plans with or without our involvement, my great desire is for neither you nor I to be bypassed by God in His workings. This is precisely why we must be people who respond to great opportunities with great faith in our great God. Remember, our God "is able, through his mighty power at work within us, to accomplish infinitely more than we might ask or think" (Ephesians 3:20, NLT).

Do we sincerely believe this? Are you and I truly convinced that with God everything is possible? I will have to admit that there have been occasions when I have been tempted to doubt and to give up on some plan, some opportunity, or at times maybe even some individual because, with my limited abilities, resources, and understanding, the situation seemed impossible. I have been guilty of thinking, "That person will never come to faith in Christ. Their heart is just too hard." Then, at other times, I have thought, "There's no way God could use me to share the Gospel with someone. I'm not a good speaker, and I don't know all of the answers."

However, Jesus offers a different perspective. In Matthew 19:26 (NLT), He declares, "Humanly speaking, (that situation) is impossible. But with God, everything is possible." Here, Jesus was conveying the same lesson to Philip and the other disciples that He continues to teach us today. Our God can accomplish a lot with just a little when we place our trust in Him.

Turning our attention back to the story, we observe another disciple entering the conversation. The Bible tells us that Andrew, Simon Peter's brother, spoke up, saying, "There's a young boy here with five barley loaves and two fish" (John 6:9, NLT).

At this moment, it almost seems as though one of Jesus' disciples was beginning to exhibit a little faith by saying, "Hey, guys, look! Here's something for us to start with." However, as Andrew continued speaking, we quickly realize this is not the case. In verse 9, he asked Jesus the question, "But what good is that with such a huge crowd?" (John 6:9, NLT). In other words, "How can this small amount of food possibly make a difference when there is such an enormous need?"

It is at this point that I sometimes wonder if this was just a lack of faith or if another kind of problem was starting to surface. Had Jesus' disciples started thinking, "Let's just keep this food for ourselves. After all, we've been out here all day ministering to the people, and we're hungry too."

Now, it might sound harsh to consider this a possibility, but we must remember that these men were human, just like us. And if we are truly honest, we would have to admit that there have been times when we have been tempted to do just that—to hold on to what we have been blessed with and consume it all ourselves. And I am not referring only to our finances. This applies to our time, our wisdom, our spiritual gifts, and more.

My friend, God is completely able to make a positive impact with everything we turn over to Him and still provide for our needs in the process. How can we be sure of this? Look back at John 6:10-11. Here we find Jesus instructing His disciples by saying, "'Tell everyone to sit down.' So they all sat down on the grassy slopes. (The men alone numbered about 5,000.) Then Jesus took the loaves, gave thanks to God, and distributed them to the people. Afterward, he did the same with the fish. And they all ate as much as they wanted" (John 6:10-11, NLT).

Apparently, this one boy was the only person, out of thousands of people, who came prepared that day. Now, I am not suggesting that he left his home that morning thinking, "I hope I can give all of my food away and feed a lot of hungry people." But for one reason or another, he arrived prepared for whatever need he might have regarding food, and he managed to take care of this very important resource (his food) until the time when it was needed.

Stewardship, as emphasized in the Bible, is not just about managing our resources but also about being prepared for the opportunities and the tasks God sets before us. Good preparation is a foundational aspect of biblical stewardship, something that God teaches His people to practice in all areas of life. In fact, as you read through the Bible, you will see how God warns us, encourages us, and instructs us regarding the benefits of being prepared as well as the downside of failing to make proper preparations.

Physical Preparation

One type of preparation God instructs His people to give attention to involves physical readiness for the future. Now, I want to clarify that I am not suggesting anyone should prioritize exercise to the point of it becoming an idol. However, what I am emphasizing is that appropriate physical preparations can enable us to lead healthier and more active lives. This, in turn, enables us to serve God more fully for as long as He desires our presence on this Earth.

In 1 Timothy 4:8 (NLT), the apostle Paul said to Timothy, "Physical training is good." My guess is that many, if not most, who are reading this book would probably say that there is something about their health or their physical condition that they wish was different. And having lived as long as I have, I am convinced that most of us could benefit from making some type of preparation for our bodies to carry us into a healthier future. However, to do this, we might have to change our eating habits, exercise a little, and even visit the doctor for regular check-ups.

As I write these words, I can easily imagine some people responding with, "I'm too busy. That's embarrassing," or "It's probably no big deal." Yet, I also believe that many of us have known at least one person in our past who might still be with us today if they had prepared for a longer, healthier life.

Spiritual Preparation

After imparting his wisdom about physical preparedness to Timothy, Paul shifted focus to a more significant aspect of readiness: spiritual preparedness. Paul elaborates on this in 1 Timothy 4:8 (NLT), where he asserts, "Physical training is good, but training for godliness is much better, promising benefits in this life and in the life to come."

By now you are probably well aware of the fact that there is an enemy who seeks to trip you up and lead you astray every day. Thankfully, God is greater, and He has equipped us with the Holy Spirit, His Word, prayer, and our church family to help us prepare for and overcome the attacks of the devil. However, having these provisions from God does not automatically guarantee that we will realize their benefits. Success requires a daily commitment to ready oneself for the spiritual battles that lie ahead.

So, how do we do this?

In Ephesians 6:14-18 (CSB), the Word of God says this:

Stand, therefore, with truth like a belt around your waist, righteousness like armor on your chest, and your feet sandaled with readiness for the gospel of peace. In every situation, take up the shield of faith with which you can extinguish all the flaming arrows of the evil one. Take the helmet of salvation and the sword of the Spirit—which is the word of God. Pray at all times in the Spirit with every prayer and request, and stay alert with all perseverance and intercession for all the saints.

Spiritual warfare is a very real and ongoing battle that we face every day. Ephesians 6:12 (NIV) says, "For our struggle is not against flesh and blood, but against the rulers, against the authorities, against the powers of this dark world and against the spiritual forces of evil in the heavenly realms." Therefore, as the Bible instructs us, we must prepare ourselves for this battle each day by "[putting] on the full armor of God" (Ephesians 6:11, CSB).

The belt of truth, the first piece of armor mentioned for Christians, holds significant symbolic meaning. It represents integrity and a strong foundation in God's truth. This primacy underscores the essential role of truth in the believer's life. Understanding and embodying God's truth is vital; without it, we are vulnerable to being swayed by "every wind of doctrine, by the trickery of men, in the cunning craftiness of deceitful plotting," as Paul warns in Ephesians 4:14 (NKJV).[22] By integrating God's truth into our daily lives, we strengthen our

[22] John MacArthur, *New Testament Commentary: Ephesians* (Chicago: Moody Publishers, 1986), 349.

ability to discern and reject falsehoods. This, in turn, enables us to live in a way that honors and pleases God in every part of our existence.

The second piece of armor Paul mentions in Ephesians is the breastplate of righteousness. "This piece of armor, made of metal plates and chains, covered the body from the neck to the waist, both front and back."[23] Just as the breastplate was essential for a Roman soldier in protecting vital organs, for Christians, it represents the righteousness of Christ shielding us from the enemy's accusations. As believers, we are called to pursue a life of righteousness by following holiness and obeying God's commands. Living in this manner enables us to effectively repel the enemy's attacks and reinforces our confidence in the salvation that is ours.

The third piece of armor is the shoes of the Gospel of peace. The shoes of the Roman soldier were equipped with hobnails that provided stability and traction in battle.[24] For us as Christians, the shoes of the Gospel represent the peace that comes from knowing Jesus as Savior and sharing the Good News about Him with others. We must be ready to share the saving message of Jesus with those around us and be peacemakers in our relationships. By doing so, we can stand firm in our faith and bring the message of hope to others.

---

[23] Warren W. Wiersbe, *The Bible Exposition Commentary, Volume 2* (Wheaton, IL: Victor Books, 1994), 58.

[24] Max Anders, *Galatians, Ephesians, Philippians, and Colossians*, vol. 8, *Holman New Testament Commentary* (Nashville: B&H Publishing Group, 1999), 191.

The fourth piece of armor is the shield of faith. This shield represents our faith in Jesus as Savior and our trust in His promises. It protects us from the fiery arrows of the enemy and enables us to remain steadfast in the face of trials and temptations. We must have faith in God's ability to protect us and guide us through all of life's challenges.

The fifth piece of the armor of God is the helmet of salvation. This crucial equipment symbolizes the assurance of our salvation, safeguarding a believer's mind from doubts, fears, and the deceptions of the enemy. "Satan is intent on convincing us to view ourselves as unloved and unlovable."[25] However, when we don the helmet of salvation, we reaffirm our identity as God's children, recalling our salvation through faith in Jesus Christ. This certainty fortifies our minds against the enemy's attacks aimed at undermining our faith and driving us toward confusion, anxiety, and despair.

The sixth piece of armor is the sword of the Spirit, which is the Word of God. This is the only offensive weapon in the armor of God, and it represents the power and authority of God's Word in our lives. "Believers need this 'sword' to combat the enemy's assault, much as Christ did three times when tempted by the devil (Matt. 4:1-11)."[26] We must read, study, and meditate on

---

[25] Larry Richards, *The Full Armor of God: Defending Your Life From Satan's Schemes* (Bloomington, MN: Chosen Books, 2013), 35.

[26] John F. Walvoord and Roy B. Zuck, eds., *The Bible Knowledge Commentary: New Testament Edition* (Wheaton, IL: Victor Books, 1983), 644.

the Word of God daily, allowing it to transform us and guide our every thought and action.

Finally, the Word of God directs us toward prayer, that crucial tool for communicating with God and seeking His guidance, strength, and protection in every facet of our lives. In his letter to the Ephesian church, Paul urged readers "to engage in persistent, Spirit-led prayers like a relentless assault."[27] This call extends beyond addressing personal needs, urging us as Christians to also intercede for others.

Living as disciples of Jesus means existing in the world without succumbing to its influences. We encounter spiritual battles daily, but God has provided us with the necessary armor to withstand the devil's schemes. Putting on the full armor of God is not a one-time event; it is a daily practice of surrendering to God and relying on Him for strength and protection. By faithfully equipping ourselves with the full armor of God each day, we are able to walk in the victory that has already been secured for us through the death, burial, and resurrection of Jesus Christ.

Financial Preparation

Another clear example of God encouraging His people to be prepared is evident in the way we are instructed to handle our finances. David reminds us in Psalm 24:1

---

[27] Bill Cook and Chuck Lawless, *Spiritual Warfare in the Storyline of Scripture* (Nashville: B&H Academic, 2019), 150.

(NLT) that "The earth is the Lord's, and everything in it." This includes not just people, plants, and animals, but also our finances. Therefore, since God owns everything, including money, we are simply managers of what He entrusts to us.[28] And part of God's plan for being prepared involves saving a portion of what we earn. Unfortunately, many people have a tendency to spend everything they make—and more. As a result, they are not prepared for unexpected expenses or for the work God desires to accomplish through their financial involvement.

However, the Bible says, "Take a lesson from the ants… Learn from their ways and become wise! Though they have no prince or governor or ruler to make them work, they labor hard all summer, gathering food for the winter" (Proverbs 6:6-8, NLT).

The Bible points out that ants—even without the advice of Dave Ramsey or any other financial advisor—prepare for the inevitable difficult times, such as winter, that lie ahead. If ants are wise enough to prepare by consuming less than what they gather, then God's people should be able to do the same.

One valuable principle I learned long ago is commonly known as the 10-10-80 Principle. This easy-to-remember guideline suggests that I should allocate the first 10% of my gross income to God through my local church. The next 10% is earmarked for savings

---

[28] Randy Alcorn, *The Treasure Principle: Unlocking the Secret of Joyful Giving*, rev. and updated (New York: Multnomah, 2022), 25.

and investments. After setting aside these portions, the remaining 80% of my income is used for living expenses. Then, as my income grows over time, it is advisable to consider increasing the amounts designated for God and savings while reducing the percentage used for living expenses.

Now, let me be clear and upfront with you about something very important. I am neither a financial planner, nor do I have a fancy program to sell you regarding budgeting, retirement, or how to gain wealth. However, something I do know, personally and powerfully, is this: In the Old Testament book of Malachi, God makes an incredible promise to His people who demonstrate their trust in Him and worship God through their finances. Here, we read the following: "I am the LORD All-Powerful, and I challenge you to put me to the test. Bring the entire ten percent into the storehouse, so there will be food in my house. Then I will open the windows of heaven and flood you with blessing after blessing" (Malachi 3:10, CEV). For those who argue that this promise is solely Old Testament and not relevant today, consider this: the underlying spiritual principle of this promise is reflected in Luke 6:38 and 2 Corinthians 9:6-8, allowing contemporary believers to embrace it as well.[29]

After Kim and I got married, we committed to trusting God and worshipping Him with the resources He

[29] Warren W. Wiersbe, *The Wiersbe Bible Commentary: The Complete Old Testament*, 2nd ed. (Colorado Springs: David C. Cook, 2007), 1531.

provided through our jobs. Even during times when finances were tight, we continued our practice of tithing and placing our trust in Him. Thankfully, we have found that God has always been faithful in His provision. He has taken care of our needs and allowed us to be a part of His eternal work through what we bring to Him.

Friend, it is important to understand that God does not need your money. God owns everything! However, as your Savior and your provider, He offers you the opportunity to worship Him and join Him in the incredible work He is doing to impact lives for eternity. When we demonstrate our love and faith by following God's instructions regarding tithing, then God does what only He can do and fulfills His promise of provision to us. So, I would encourage anyone who is not currently tithing to trust God and to worship Him with your finances and experience what God will do.

Ponder and Practice

1. **Faith Impacts Finances and Vice Versa:** Reflect on the connection between your faith and your finances. How has your spiritual journey influenced your financial decisions and vice versa? Discuss the concept of stewardship and how viewing your resources as God's provision can change your approach to managing them.
2. **Preparing for the Future:** This chapter emphasizes the importance of both physical and spiritual preparation. Share your strategies for maintaining physical health as a form of stewardship. Similarly, discuss how you equip yourself spiritually each day (e.g., prayer, Bible study) to face life's challenges.
3. **The 10-10-80 Principle in Financial Stewardship:** Reflect on your financial practices in relation to the 10-10-80 Principle (allocating 10% to God, saving 10%, and living on the remaining 80%). Discuss the challenges and benefits of this principle, and plan steps to align your financial habits with this model.

4. **Openness to God's Prompting:** Reflect on the story of the boy who shared his lunch with Jesus. Discuss the significance of being open to God's prompting in seemingly small acts of contribution. How can we cultivate a heart that is responsive to using whatever we have, no matter how insignificant it may seem, for God's purposes? Share thoughts on how this principle can be applied in various aspects of life, such as time, talents, and resources.
5. **Tithing as an Act of Worship and Trust:** Share your perspectives on tithing as an act of worship and trust in God. How does practicing financial stewardship, such as tithing, reflect your faith and reliance on Him? Discuss any experiences or insights regarding how managing your finances has influenced your spiritual journey.

Chapter 8
Well Done

Well done, good and faithful servant.

–Matthew 25:23, NLT

AS YOU COME to the close of this book, I want to remind you of the importance of pressing on in your walk with Jesus. The Christian life is not just about a one-time decision, but a lifelong journey of faith, growth, and transformation. As the apostle Paul says, "I press on to reach the end of the race and receive the heavenly prize for which God, through Christ Jesus, is calling us" (Philippians 3:14, NLT).

In order to press on and run the race well, it is important to remember the foundational principles that you have learned in this book. We have discussed the importance of identifying with Jesus through baptism, sharing the Gospel, joining a Bible-believing church, knowing the Word of God, communicating with God, worshipping Him, and being good stewards of what He has entrusted to us. These are all crucial aspects of the Christian life that must be continually pursued and developed.

As you press on, it is important to remember that you are not alone on this journey. God has given us His Holy Spirit to guide and empower us. As Jesus Himself promised, "I am with you always, even to the end of the age" (Matthew 28:20, NLT). He is our strength, our source of hope, and He will never leave us.

Staying deeply connected to God's Word is also crucial. As the psalmist expressed, "Your word is a lamp to guide my feet and a light for my path" (Psalm 119:105, NLT). Through regular reading and memorization of the Bible, we can gain wisdom and guidance for our lives. This practice also brings encouragement to press on, especially in challenging times, as we are continually reminded of God's promises and His steadfast faithfulness to us.

Lastly, staying connected to a community of believers is essential. As Hebrews 10:24-25 (NLT) urges, "Let us think of ways to motivate one another to acts of love and good works. And let us not neglect our meeting together, as some people do, but encourage one another, especially now that the day of his return is drawing near." We need to give and receive the encouragement and support that can only be found in a community of faith known as the local church.

So, my friend, as you press on in this race toward your heavenly prize, remember: Jesus is with you, His

Word is your guide, and His church is your community. May you continue to grow in your love for Him and your desire to serve Him until that day when He speaks those precious words to you, "Well done, good and faithful servant" (Matthew 25:23, NLT).

Appendix A
Writing Your Salvation Story

Take a few minutes to write out your story of becoming a Christian. This is the beginning of your testimony and will be a powerful tool as you start to share Jesus with others in your life. The following is an outline to help you write your personal faith story.

1. Your life before Jesus.
   a. Where were you spiritually before receiving Christ, and how did that affect you—your feelings, attitudes, actions, and relationships?
   b. What caused you to begin considering Jesus as your Savior?
2. How you came to Jesus.
   a. What realization did you come to that finally motivated you to trust in Jesus?
   b. Specifically, how did you receive Jesus as your Savior?

3. Your life since becoming a Christian.
    a. How did your life begin to change after you placed your faith in Jesus?
    b. What other benefits have you experienced since becoming a Christian?

As you write, remember:

- Be concise and simple in wording.
- Avoid religious clichés or words and phrases that are not easily understood.
- Be direct and to the point.
- Make it 2 to 4 minutes in length.
- Emphasize aspects of your story that will relate to the person you are talking to.

Appendix B

The Four Spiritual Laws

The following are a few conversation starters that can help you jump-start a Gospel conversation.

Option 1:

"Friend, as you know, I don't claim to be a perfect person, but I was wondering if I could tell you about someone who really helped me."

Option 2:

"I used to worry about what's next (what comes after this life), but then I discovered something that made a difference and gave me great peace. I was wondering if I could share my story with you."

Option 3:

"There seems to be so much evil going on around us, and I was wondering if I could share with you the source of my strength and peace."

Once you have a person's permission to proceed, walk them through the following conversational outline by saying the following.

The first truth I want to make sure is clear is that:

1. God loves you and has a wonderful plan for you.

God loved the people of this world so much that he gave his only Son. –John 3:16, CEV

You're a part of this world, so that means God loves you! But, while it's true that God loves you, there is also an enemy that wants to harm you.

The thief comes only to steal and kill and destroy. I came that they may have life and have it abundantly. –John 10:10, ESV

Jesus is not some cosmic killjoy. He came to give you the best life you could ever hope for—the blessed life that God created you to live.

However, there is a very big problem. The Bible says:

2. Our sin separates us from God and His blessed plan for us.

All of us have sinned. –Romans 3:23, CEV

No human is perfect. All of us have sinned, and our sin does something terrible to us. It separates us from God and His perfect, eternal Kingdom.

Your iniquities have separated you from your God; your sins have hidden his face from you, so that he will not hear. –Isaiah 59:2, NIV

If a person leaves this earth in that unforgiven and separated condition, then that is how they will spend eternity—separated from God's Kingdom in a very real place called Hell.

But, God loves us, and He does not want that for anyone. So, He did the only thing that could be done to help us.

3. God sent His Son Jesus as the one and only sacrifice He would accept for the forgiveness of our sins.

Jesus [said], "I am the way, the truth, and the life. No one can come to the Father except through me." –John 14:6, NLT

A lot of people have a lot of opinions about how they can get to Heaven, but the Son of God made it very, very clear. He is the only way to God.

Christ suffered for our sins once for all time. He never sinned, but he died for sinners to bring you safely home to God. –1 Peter 3:18, NLT

When Jesus died upon the cross, He experienced the suffering and the separation we deserve.

For the wages of sin is death, but the free gift of God is eternal life through Christ Jesus our Lord. –Romans 6:23, NLT

God offers this free gift of forgiveness and an eternal home in Heaven to everyone.

But, like any gift, it only becomes yours when you receive it. And that is true with the gift of His forgiveness.

4. God's forgiveness and eternal blessings become ours when we place our faith in Jesus.

> *God saved you by his grace when you believed. And you can't take credit for this; it is a gift from God. Salvation is not a reward for the good things we have done, so none of us can boast about it.* –Ephesians 2:8-9, NLT

> *If you confess with your mouth, 'Jesus is Lord,' and believe in your heart that God raised him from the dead, you will be saved.* –Romans 10:9, CSB

Friend, would you like to receive the gift of God's forgiveness, have His help for your life today, and know that you have an eternal home in Heaven waiting for you? If so, then with faith in Jesus, pray the following prayer:

> *"God, I admit that I am a sinner separated from You. But I know that You love me. I believe that Jesus died on the cross for my forgiveness, and then He rose from the grave so I could have eternal life. Now, Jesus, I am trusting in You. Be my Savior and forgive me of my sins. With Your help, I will follow You as my Lord all the days of my life. Thank You, God, for saving*

me now and forever more. This is my prayer in Jesus' name. Amen."

Be sure to invite this new Christian to church. Give them a copy of this book. If possible, also make plans for ongoing encouragement and follow-up.

Appendix C
Basic Beliefs

The following contains portions of the Baptist Faith and Message 2000.[30]

The Scriptures

The Holy Bible was written by men divinely inspired and is the record of God's revelation of Himself to man. It is a perfect treasure of divine instruction. It has God for its author, salvation for its end, and truth, without any mixture of error, for its matter. Therefore, all Scripture is totally true and trustworthy. It reveals the principles by which God judges us, and therefore is, and will remain to the end of the world, the true center of Christian union, and the supreme standard by which all human conduct, creeds, and religious opinions should

[30] Southern Baptist Convention, *Baptist Faith and Message 2000*, sec. II, accessed September 28, 2023, https://bfm.sbc.net/bfm2000/#ii.

be tried. All scripture is a testimony to Christ, who is Himself the focus of divine revelation.

Exodus 24:4; Deuteronomy 4:1-2; 17:19; Joshua 8:34; Psalms 19:7-10; 119:11,89,105,140; Isaiah 34:16; 40:8; Jeremiah 15:16; 36:1-32; Matthew 5:17-18; 22:29; Luke 21:33; 24:44-46; John 5:39; 16:13-15; 17:17; Acts 2:16ff.; 17:11; Romans 15:4; 16:25-26; 2 Timothy 3:15-17; Hebrews 1:1-2; 4:12; 1 Peter 1:25; 2 Peter 1:19-21

The Trinity

There is one and only one living and true God. He is an intelligent, spiritual, and personal Being, the Creator, Redeemer, Preserver, and Ruler of the universe. God is infinite in holiness and all other perfections. God is all-powerful and all-knowing; and His perfect knowledge extends to all things, past, present, and future, including the future decisions of His free creatures. To Him we owe the highest love, reverence, and obedience. The eternal triune God reveals Himself to us as Father, Son, and Holy Spirit, with distinct personal attributes, but without division of nature, essence, or being.

God the Father

God as Father reigns with providential care over His universe, His creatures, and the flow of the stream of human history according to the purposes of His grace. He is all-powerful, all-knowing, all-loving, and all-wise.

God is Father in truth to those who become children of God through faith in Jesus Christ. He is fatherly in His attitude toward all men.

Genesis 1:1; 2:7; Exodus 3:14; 6:2-3; 15:11ff.; 20:1ff.; Leviticus 22:2; Deuteronomy 6:4; 32:6; 1 Chronicles 29:10; Psalm 19:1-3; Isaiah 43:3,15; 64:8; Jeremiah 10:10; 17:13; Matthew 6:9ff.; 7:11; 23:9; 28:19; Mark 1:9-11; John 4:24; 5:26; 14:6-13; 17:1-8; Acts 1:7; Romans 8:14-15; 1 Corinthians 8:6; Galatians 4:6; Ephesians 4:6; Colossians 1:15; 1 Timothy 1:17; Hebrews 11:6; 12:9; 1 Peter 1:17; 1 John 5:7

God the Son

Christ is the eternal Son of God. In His incarnation as Jesus Christ He was conceived of the Holy Spirit and born of the virgin Mary. Jesus perfectly revealed and did the will of God, taking upon Himself human nature with its demands and necessities and identifying Himself completely with mankind yet without sin. He honored the divine law by His personal obedience, and in His substitutionary death on the cross He made provision for the redemption of men from sin. He was raised from the dead with a glorified body and appeared to His disciples as the person who was with them before His crucifixion. He ascended into heaven and is now exalted at the right hand of God where He is the One Mediator, fully God, fully man, in whose Person is effected the reconciliation between God and man. He will return in power and glory to judge the world and to consummate His redemptive mission. He now dwells in all believers as the living and ever-present Lord.

Genesis 18:1ff.; Psalms 2:7ff.; 110:1ff.; Isaiah 7:14; Isaiah 53:1-12; Matthew 1:18-23; 3:17; 8:29; 11:27; 14:33; 16:16,27; 17:5; 27; 28:1-6,19; Mark 1:1; 3:11; Luke 1:35; 4:41; 22:70; 24:46; John 1:1-18,29; 10:30,38; 11:25-27; 12:44-50; 14:7-11; 16:15-16,28; 17:1-5, 21-22; 20:1-20,28; Acts 1:9; 2:22-24; 7:55-56; 9:4-5,20; Romans 1:3-4; 3:23-26; 5:6-21; 8:1-3,34; 10:4; 1 Corinthians 1:30; 2:2; 8:6; 15:1-8,24-28; 2 Corinthians 5:19-21; 8:9; Galatians 4:4-5; Ephesians 1:20; 3:11; 4:7-10; Philippians 2:5-11; Colossians 1:13-22; 2:9; 1 Thessalonians 4:14-18; 1 Timothy 2:5-6; 3:16; Titus 2:13-14; Hebrews 1:1-3; 4:14-15; 7:14-28; 9:12-15,24-28; 12:2; 13:8; 1 Peter 2:21-25; 3:22; 1 John 1:7-9; 3:2; 4:14-15; 5:9; 2 John 7-9; Revelation 1:13-16; 5:9-14; 12:10-11; 13:8; 19:16

God the Holy Spirit

The Holy Spirit is the Spirit of God, fully divine. He inspired holy men of old to write the Scriptures. Through illumination, He enables men to understand truth. He exalts Christ. He convicts of sin, of righteousness and of judgment. He calls men to the Savior, and effects regeneration. At the moment of regeneration, He baptizes every believer into the Body of Christ. He cultivates Christian character, comforts believers and bestows the spiritual gifts by which they serve God through His church. He seals the believer unto the day of final redemption. His presence in the Christian is the guarantee that God will bring the believer into the fullness of the stature of Christ. He enlightens and empowers the believer and the church in worship, evangelism, and service.

Genesis 1:2; Judges 14:6; Job 26:13; Psalms 51:11; 139:7ff.; Isaiah 61:1-3; Joel 2:28- 32; Matthew 1:18; 3:16; 4:1; 12:28-32; 28:19; Mark 1:10, 12; Luke 1:35; 4:1, 18-19; 11:13; 12:12; 24:49; John 4:24; 14:16-17, 26; 15:26; 16:7-14; Acts 1:8; 2:1-4, 38; 4:31; 5:3; 6:3; 7:55; 8:17, 39; 10:44; 13:2; 15:28; 16:6; 19:1-6; Romans 8:9-11, 14-16, 26-27; 1 Corinthians 2:10-14; 3:16; 12:3-11, 13; Galatians 4:6; Ephesians 1:13-14; 4:30; 5:18; 1 Thessalonians 5:19; 1 Timothy 3:16; 4:1; 2 Timothy 1:14; 3:16; Hebrews 9:8, 14; 2 Peter 1:21; 1 John 4:13; 5:6-7; Revelation 1:10; 22:17

Man

Man is the special creation of God, made in His own image. He created them male and female as the crowning work of His creation. The gift of gender is thus part of the goodness of God's creation. In the beginning man was innocent of sin and was endowed by his Creator with freedom of choice. By his free choice man sinned against God and brought sin into the human race. Through the temptation of Satan man transgressed the command of God, and fell from his original innocence whereby his posterity inherited a nature and an environment inclined toward sin. Therefore, as soon as they are capable of moral action, they become transgressors and are under condemnation. Only the grace of God can bring man into His holy fellowship and enable man to fulfill the creative purpose of God. The sacredness of human personality is evident in that God created man in His own image, and in that Christ died for man; therefore, every person of every race possesses full dignity and is worthy of respect and Christian love.

Genesis 1:26-30; 2:5,7,18-22; 3; 9:6; Psalms 1; 8:3-6; 32:1-5; 51:5; Isaiah 6:5; Jeremiah 17:5; Matthew 16:26; Acts 17:26-31; Romans 1:19-32; 3:10-18,23; 5:6,12,19; 6:6; 7:14-25; 8:14-18,29; 1 Corinthians 1:21-31; 15:19,21-22; Ephesians 2:1-22; Colossians 1:21-22; 3:9-11

Salvation

Salvation involves the redemption of the whole man, and is offered freely to all who accept Jesus Christ as Lord and Savior, who by His own blood obtained eternal redemption for the believer. In its broadest sense salvation includes regeneration, justification, sanctification, and glorification. There is no salvation apart from personal faith in Jesus Christ as Lord.

1. Regeneration, or the new birth, is a work of God's grace whereby believers become new creatures in Christ Jesus. It is a change of

heart wrought by the Holy Spirit through conviction of sin, to which the sinner responds in repentance toward God and faith in the Lord Jesus Christ. Repentance and faith are inseparable experiences of grace.

Repentance is a genuine turning from sin toward God. Faith is the acceptance of Jesus Christ and commitment of the entire personality to Him as Lord and Savior.

2. Justification is God's gracious and full acquittal upon principles of His righteousness of all sinners who repent and believe in Christ. Justification brings the believer unto a relationship of peace and favor with God.
3. Sanctification is the experience, beginning in regeneration, by which the believer is set apart to God's purposes, and is enabled to progress toward moral and spiritual maturity through the presence and power of the Holy Spirit dwelling in him. Growth in grace should continue throughout the regenerate person's life.
4. Glorification is the culmination of salvation and is the final blessed and abiding state of the redeemed.

Genesis 3:15; Exodus 3:14-17; 6:2-8; Matthew 1:21; 4:17; 16:21-26; 27:22-28:6; Luke 1:68-69; 2:28-32; John 1:11-14,29; 3:3-21,36; 5:24; 10:9,28-29; 15:1-16; 17:17; Acts 2:21; 4:12; 15:11; 16:30-31;

17:30-31; 20:32; Romans 1:16-18; 2:4; 3:23-25; 4:3ff.; 5:8-10; 6:1-23; 8:1-18,29-39; 10:9-10,13; 13:11-14; 1 Corinthians 1:18,30; 6:19-20; 15:10; 2 Corinthians 5:17-20; Galatians 2:20; 3:13; 5:22-25; 6:15; Ephesians 1:7; 2:8-22; 4:11-16; Philippians 2:12-13; Colossians 1:9-22; 3:1ff.; 1 Thessalonians 5:23-24; 2 Timothy 1:12; Titus 2:11-14; Hebrews 2:1-3; 5:8-9; 9:24-28; 11:1-12:8,14; James 2:14-26; 1 Peter 1:2-23; 1 John 1:6-2:11; Revelation 3:20; 21:1-22:5

The Family

God has ordained the family as the foundational institution of human society. It is composed of persons related to one another by marriage, blood, or adoption.

Marriage is the uniting of one man and one woman in covenant commitment for a lifetime. It is God's unique gift to reveal the union between Christ and His church and to provide for the man and the woman in marriage the framework for intimate companionship, the channel of sexual expression according to biblical standards, and the means for procreation of the human race.

Children, from the moment of conception, are a blessing and heritage from the Lord. Parents are to demonstrate to their children God's pattern for marriage. Parents are to teach their children spiritual and moral values and to lead them, through consistent lifestyle example and loving discipline, to make choices based on biblical truth. Children are to honor and obey their parents.

Genesis 1:26-28; 2:15-25; 3:1-20; Exodus 20:12; Deuteronomy 6:4-9; Joshua 24:15; 1 Samuel 1:26-28; Psalms 51:5; 78:1-8; Psalms 127; Psalms 128; 139:13-16; Proverbs 1:8; 5:15-20; 6:20-22; 12:4; 13:24; 14:1; 17:6; 18:22; 22:6,15; 23:13-14; 24:3; 29:15,17; 31:10-31; Ecclesiastes 4:9-12; 9:9; Malachi 2:14-16; Matthew 5:31-32; 18:2-5; 19:3-9; Mark 10:6-12; Romans 1:18-32; 1 Corinthians 7:1-16; Ephesians 5:21-33; 6:1-4; Colossians 3:18-21; 1 Timothy 5:8,14; 2 Timothy 1:3-5; Titus 2:3-5; Hebrews 13:4; 1 Peter 3:1-7

Bibliography

Alcorn, Randy. *The Treasure Principle: Unlocking the Secret of Joyful Giving.* Revised and updated. New York: Multnomah, 2022.

Calvin, John. *Institutes Of The Christian Religion, Book Fourth.* Houston: V Solas Press, 2021.

Cambridge Dictionary. "Supplication." Accessed May 12, 2021. https://dictionary.cambridge.org/us/dictionary/english/supplication.

Cook, Bill, and Chuck Lawless. *Spiritual Warfare in the Storyline of Scripture.* Nashville: B&H Academic, 2019.

Evans, Tony. *Tony Evans' Book of Illustrations: Stories, Quotes, and Anecdotes From More Than 30 Years of Preaching and Public Speaking.* Chicago: Moody Publishers, 2009.

Foreman, George, and Ken Abraham. *God In My Corner.* Nashville: Thomas Nelson, 2007.

Gibbons, James. "The Faith Of Our Fathers." *The Project Gutenberg*, 2008. Accessed May 12, 2023. https://www.gutenberg.org/cache/epub/27435/pg27435-images.html.

Graham, Billy. *Peace with God: The Secret of Happiness.* Nashville: Harper Collins Publishers, 1953, 1984.

Kinnaman, David. "Is Evangelism Going Out of Style?" Barna. Accessed February 16, 2022. https://www.barna.com/research/is-evangelism-going-out-of-style/.

Lockyer, Herbert, Sr., ed. *Illustrated Bible Dictionary.* Nashville: Thomas Nelson, 1986. s.v. "Baptism."

Luther, Martin. *Luther's Three Treatises.* Moscow, ID: Canon Press, 2021.

MacArthur, John. *Ephesians.* Chicago: Moody Publishers, 1986.

Anders, Max. *Galatians, Ephesians, Philippians, and Colossians.* Vol. 8 of *Holman New Testament Commentary.* Nashville: B&H Publishing Group, 1999.

Moore, Henry. *Life of the Reverend John Wesley, A.M., fellow of Lincoln College, Oxford.* New-York: N. Bangs and J. Emory, 1824. J. & J. Harper and A. Hoyt imprint. Accessed June 28, 2023. https://go.gale.com/ps/i.do?p=SABN&u=vic_liberty&id=GALE|CY0111260895&v=2.1&it=r&sid=summon.

Phelan, James. *Howard Hughes: The Hidden Years.* New York: Random House, 1976.

Reid, Alvin L. *Sharing Jesus without Freaking Out.* Nashville: B&H Academic, 2017.

Richards, Larry. *The Full Armor of God: Defending Your Life From Satan's Schemes.* Bloomington, Minnesota: Chosen Books, 2013.

Rinker, Rosalind. *Prayer: Conversing With God.* Grand Rapids: Zondervan Publishing House, 1959.

RWD. "Grass On Your Path." Our Daily Bread, November 18, 1996.

Southern Baptist Convention. *Baptist Faith and Message 2000.* Accessed September 28, 2023. https://bfm.sbc.net/bfm2000/#ii.

"Supplication." Cambridge Dictionary. Accessed May 12, 2021. https://dictionary.cambridge.org/us/dictionary/english/supplication.

Walvoord, John F., and Roy B. Zuck, eds. *The Bible Knowledge Commentary: New Testament Edition.* Wheaton, IL: Victor Books, 1983.

Wesley, John. *John Wesley,* edited by A. C. Outler. Oxford University Press, Incorporated, 1980. ProQuest Ebook Central. Accessed June 28, 2023. http://ebookcentral.proquest.com/lib/liberty/detail.action?docID=684619.

Wesley, John. *John Wesley's Notes On Paul's Epistle To The Romans.* Nashville: Methodist Evangelistic Materials, 1962.

"What You Can't See, Can Hurt You." Concrete Raising Systems. Accessed October 19, 2021. https://www.liftyourconcrete.com/what-you-cant-see-can-hurt-you/.

"Why Is Giving Thanks To God Important?" Got Questions Ministries. Accessed June 11, 2022. https://www.gotquestions.org/giving-thanks-to-God.html.

Wiersbe, Warren W. *The Wiersbe Bible Commentary: The Complete Old Testament.* 2nd ed. Colorado Springs: David C. Cook, 2007.

Wiersbe, Warren W. *The Bible Exposition Commentary, Volume 2.* Wheaton, IL: Victor Books, 1994.

Smietana, Bob. "Young Bible Readers More Likely to Be Faithful Adults, Study Finds." LifeWay Research. Accessed October 17, 2017. https://lifewayresearch.com/2017/10/17/young-bible-readers-more-likely-to-be-faithful-adults-study-finds/.

Made in the USA
Columbia, SC
19 March 2024

33117082R00088